THE FOUNDATION

Building a Real Estate Career That Stands Strong

Dani Landers

Willowcross Consulting

COPYRIGHT PAGE

ISBN-13: 979-8-9956407-2-1

Willowcross Consulting www.willowcrossconsulting.com

Printed in the United States of America Third Edition, 2026

DEDICATION

For every agent who has sat in their car between appointments wondering if they're doing this right.

You are. You just need a foundation.

PREFACE

This book was written for real estate agents who want more than survival.

It was written for agents who want a business that supports their life, not consumes it. For agents who want to understand how to use what's already around them to do their job well, consistently, and professionally.

Most real estate resources focus on either sales skills or compliance. They tell you which forms to use, what scripts to memorize, or how to close a deal. Those things matter. But they don't explain how all the moving parts of this business fit together in real life.

As an agent, you are surrounded by systems, people, tools, and support. Teams, brokerages, CRMs, transaction coordinators, marketing platforms, data, and processes exist to help you. The challenge is that no one teaches you how to apply them intentionally.

The Foundation was created to fill that gap.

This book goes beyond what to do and focuses on how to operate:

- How to structure your time
- How to use systems instead of memory
- How to lean on leverage without losing control
- How to understand the numbers without fear
- How to build consistency regardless of market conditions

If you are on a team, this book helps you take full advantage of the specialized support around you while you build skill and confidence. If you are a solo agent, it helps you create that structure deliberately using tools and discipline. Leverage on a team has a person in a role. Solo, this role may be a system or automation. Leverage comes through people or process. The principles are the same. The application may differ.

This book is not about working harder. It is about working with clarity.

A strong foundation doesn't make the job easy. It makes it manageable, repeatable, and sustainable. That is the foundation this book is here to help you build.

Table of Contents

PART IV — THE LONG VIEW - 135

Closing: Build Once, Adjust Often - 182

Appendices - 184

Glossary of Terms -234
About the Authors -241

HOW TO USE THIS BOOK

This book is not designed to be read quickly. It is designed to be used deliberately.

The Foundation tells its story through Mason Reyes — a new agent learning what it actually takes to build a business that holds. His experience is yours. The lessons he absorbs across four parts of this book are the same ones that determine whether an agent's career eventually steadies or quietly cracks.

Reading it as a parable is intentional. Stories teach what instruction alone cannot. When Mason sits across from Charlotte and finally understands the difference between activity and a foundation, something shifts — not because he memorized a framework, but because he lived through the moment. Read alongside him. Let the lessons land the same way.

The book is organized into four parts:

Part I — Pouring the Foundation establishes clarity and stability. Numbers, structure, time, relationships — the things most agents skip because they're not exciting, and the things that make everything else possible. (Weeks 1-3)

Part II — Framing the Business creates flow through systems and process. Once the ground is solid, Part II connects your actions so that effort compounds instead of evaporates. (Weeks 4-6)

Part III — Weight-Bearing Growth prepares your business to carry more. This is where structure is tested — and where leverage, boundaries, and delegation become strategic tools, not reactions to overwhelm. (Weeks 7-9)

Part IV — The Long View ensures a business that lasts. Not just functional, but aligned — with your life, your values, and the kind of career you actually want to sustain. (Weeks 10-12)

This book is structured to support a 12-week reading journey. That pace is not arbitrary. The concepts build on each other, and the practices they introduce take time to absorb and apply. Rushing through them produces insight without traction. Moving through them deliberately produces change.

Each week, read your chapters. Then stop. Reflect on what Mason encountered and where you see yourself in it. Ask the honest questions: Where is my foundation holding? Where is it not?

This book works best when paired with:

- **Weekly reflection** — at the end of each reading week, spend time with the questions the chapters raise. Write things down. What you put on paper becomes real in a way that thoughts alone do not.
- **Consistent routines** — the principles here don't activate through understanding. They activate through repetition. Give them a place in your schedule.
- **Willingness to adjust instead of restart** — not every section will hit at the right moment. Some concepts will feel premature; return to them later. Some will land harder than expected; sit with those.

The appendices are execution tools, not afterthoughts. Return to them often — when you're calculating your burn rate, mapping your commission flow, or auditing your CRM. They are built to support the work the chapters describe, and they hold up better on the second and third visit than they do on the first.

This is not a finish line. It is a foundation you continue to build on. Mason's story ends at a beginning — the moment the structure is solid enough to trust. Your story starts there too.

Use the structure, tools, and people around you. Use the systems and frameworks to create that structure intentionally.

Then keep building.

PART I — POURING THE FOUNDATION

Laying the groundwork for a business that can withstand the weight of growth

* * *

Part I is about building what most agents never see until it breaks: the foundation.

When a business is new, adrenaline can hide a lot of cracks. Hustle covers unclear numbers. Charisma covers a weak buyer or seller process. Late nights cover the lack of a real, living CRM. In the moment, it feels like "this is just what it takes." But underneath the activity, there is a simple question that eventually demands an answer: can this hold more weight, or is everything balanced on the edge of burnout?

A real estate business doesn't collapse because someone forgets a clever script. It cracks where the load is heaviest: in the money that's never clearly counted, the relationships that quietly drift away, and the days that are run by whatever feels loudest instead of what truly matters. Early wins can make those cracks easy to ignore. A hot streak or a strong year can convince you that sprinting is a strategy. Then the market shifts, life changes, or volume spikes — and suddenly, the same habits that once "worked" can't carry the new weight.

This first part of the book is designed to make sure that moment never catches you off guard. It trades bravado for math, memory for systems, and random effort for intentional structure. Here, you will slow down long enough to see four things clearly: what it costs you to exist each month, where your commission goes, how your time is truly being used, and whether your relationships are anchored in a living CRM or floating loosely in your phone. None of that is glamorous. All of it is structural.

Pouring the foundation is not about becoming busier. It is about becoming strongly anchored. When you know your burn rate, you stop guessing "how many deals you need" and start making decisions from facts instead of fear. When your CRM holds every relationship and next step, you stop waking up worried about who you forgot. When your calendar reflects priorities instead of emergencies, you stop confusing urgency with importance. Each of these shifts removes a little more fragility from your business and replaces it with something sturdier: predictability.

You may be tempted to jump ahead to the chapters on growth, price point, or marketing. Resist that urge. The business you are about to build will only be as strong as the foundation you pour here. In these chapters, you will be asked to look directly at the parts of the business that most agents avoid — numbers, structure, discipline — not to restrict your freedom, but to protect it. Freedom without a foundation becomes chaos. Freedom with a foundation becomes a choice.

Part I is where you choose what kind of business you are building: one that needs a constant sprint to survive, or one that can calmly support whatever you decide to place on top of it. This is the work most people skip. It is also the work that makes everything that follows sustainable.

* * *

CHAPTER 1

The Moment Everything Shifts

"Success begins the moment you stop drifting and decide to build on purpose."

* * *

Mason Reyes had been licensed for eight months when reality finally caught up with him.

He was working hard. Just not well.

He could script a buyer consultation in his sleep. He could calculate due diligence fees faster than most new agents in his office. He could talk about interest rates, new construction timelines, and HOA structures without blinking. He knew which neighborhoods flooded in hurricane season and which ones the locals actually loved. He knew the marsh views from the good units and the cut-through roads that saved ten minutes at rush hour.

But nothing he did turned into momentum.

Clients slipped away. Referrals fizzled. Opportunities went cold before they went anywhere at all.

His calendar was full. His phone buzzed constantly. He had a few closings under his belt — enough to convince himself he was doing the work. From the outside, things looked fine.

From the inside, it felt fragile.

Every win required a sprint. He'd pour everything into a transaction, close it, exhale — and then look up to find a nearly empty pipeline waiting for him on the other side. Every slow week brought a particular kind of dread: the kind that starts in the stomach and spreads. Nothing felt repeatable. Nothing felt anchored. There was no flywheel, no compounding momentum, no sense that this week's effort was building anything that would support next month.

He was sprinting constantly and somehow never getting ahead.

That realization hit hardest the Thursday morning Charlotte called him into her office.

* * *

Charlotte Reed was the team's rainmaker and team leader. She wasn't just the top producer — she was the architect of the business itself.

She lived squarely in the visionary role. She drove direction. She set standards. She built models that other people could step into and succeed within. Her job wasn't to sell every house. It was to create a business that could sell homes consistently, with or without her direct involvement in every transaction.

She didn't micromanage. She didn't rescue. She believed people rose to the level of the structure around them. Give someone a clear framework and real expectations, and they generally rise to meet them. Leave them in ambiguity, and most will default to the path of least resistance — which is almost always activity without direction.

That Thursday morning, she didn't look frustrated with Mason. She didn't look disappointed.

She looked observant.

"Mason," she said, "you're doing the work. But you're not building a business."

The words struck harder than he expected. He'd been bracing for a conversation about results — about the gap between his activity and his closings, about what he needed to do differently. He hadn't expected her to name something deeper.

"I don't understand," he said quietly.

Charlotte folded her hands on her desk.

"You're consistent at being inconsistent. You're busy without direction. And you're waiting for business instead of generating it."

Mason felt a slow, heavy sinking in his stomach — the particular feeling of recognizing a truth you've been avoiding.

"I thought the activity was the work," he said.

"Activity is the surface," Charlotte replied. "The work underneath — the systems, the financial clarity, the habits that compound — that's what turns activity into a business." She paused. "Without that, you're building on sand. You might have a good month, but you can't predict it, repeat it, or sustain it."

Mason looked out the window for a moment. The marina stretched past the parking lot, the sailboats rocking gently in their slips. He'd grown up around this coastline. He'd gotten his license because he loved this place and wanted to help people plant roots in it. He hadn't expected to spend his first year feeling like he was treading water in plain sight of the shore.

"So, what do I do?" he asked.

A small smile touched Charlotte's face.

"You learn the foundation that creates producers. And you start by meeting with Elias."

She leaned forward.

"Here's the truth most agents don't hear early enough. This business can be built solo, or it can be built on a team. Both paths work. But teams exist for one reason: to shorten the learning curve and reduce unnecessary failure while you're still learning."

She gestured toward the hallway. "This team wasn't built to replace your effort. It was built to replace the guesswork. Operations, client care, systems, standards — those aren't crutches. They're scaffolding. You're supposed to use them."

Mason nodded slowly.

"Whether you're on a team or not," Charlotte continued, "the principles are the same. You need lead generation, skill mastery, financial discipline, and accountability. Being on a team gives you guardrails while you're building those things for yourself. Take the guardrails seriously."

She picked up the phone on her desk and dialed an extension.

"He's ready for your help," she said simply, and hung up.

Mason hesitated in the doorway. He felt the weight of what was shifting in the room — not pressure exactly, but something like recognition. Like a version of himself he hadn't yet been coming into focus.

"Why now?" he asked. "You've been watching this for months. Why today?"

Charlotte looked at him with something steady in her eyes.

"Because," she said, "you finally want to hear it."

And that was the moment everything shifted.

* * *

He walked down the hall toward the operations office. The afternoon light cut across the floors in long amber stripes. The coastal air drifted through the cracked window at the end of the corridor — salt, pine, and the faint smell of low tide that defined every fall afternoon on the North Carolina coast.

Elias Bennett looked up from his desk. He pushed his glasses up his nose and smiled like he'd been waiting for this exact conversation.

"Come on in," he said gently. "Let's rebuild your foundation."

Elias wasn't a salesperson. He wasn't a rainmaker or a charismatic closer. He was something rarer in this business: the stabilizer. The operations mind who turned goals into systems and systems into reality. While Charlotte envisioned the machine, Elias made sure it ran smoothly every single day.

He oversaw operations: listings from intake to close, marketing timelines, deadlines, workflows, and the thousand small details that kept the team's client experience from fraying at the edges. He'd built the CRM structure, the transaction checklists, the vendor relationships, and the financial review rhythms that the team had come to depend on.

Not because complexity was the goal. But because simplicity, done well, requires a skeleton underneath it.

Mason sat down.

"Charlotte said I need a foundation," he said. "I'm not entirely sure what that means."

Elias nodded. He'd heard versions of this conversation many times before. New agents, talented agents, sometimes even experienced agents who'd been doing it by instinct for years — all of them arriving at this same juncture eventually. The moment when hustle ran out of runway.

"Let me ask you something," Elias said. "When you had a good month, did you know why?"

Mason thought. "Because I worked hard. Got some good leads."

"And when you had a slow month?"

"I worked less hard. The leads dried up."

Elias tilted his head. "Do you see the problem?"

Mason didn't answer.

"The common denominator in both explanations is something you have no control over," Elias said. "'Worked hard' and 'good leads' are not levers you can reliably pull. They're conditions you either have or you don't. There's no formula. No reproducibility. No way to predict next month from this one."

He picked up a pen and set it on the desk between them.

"A foundation is the set of habits, systems, and disciplines that make your results predictable regardless of conditions. When you have a foundation, a slow month is a data point — not a disaster. You know what input created it, and you know what to adjust. When you don't have a foundation, every slow month feels like evidence that real estate might not work for you."

Mason was quiet for a moment.

"I've had a few of those months," he said.

"I know," Elias replied. "That's why Charlotte sent you here."

He pulled out a fresh notebook and set it open on the desk.

"Here's where we start," Elias said. "Not with leads. Not with your script. Not with your listing presentation. We start with the truth about what it costs you to exist — and what it costs you to grow." He looked Mason in the eye.

"You don't need more leads right now. You need clarity. Structure. Habits that compound instead of scatter. You need a foundation."

Outside the window, a pelican drifted low over the marina, wings outstretched, effortless in the updraft off the water. The tide was coming in.

 Mason picked up his pen.

"Okay," he said. "Let's build it."

* * *

FOUNDATION MARKER

Leadership Window: Support Is Not a Shortcut

High-performing teams don't remove responsibility — they provide structure while responsibility is being learned. When an agent finally decides to build intentionally, the support already around them becomes useful in a way it never was before. Charlotte's scaffolding had always been there. Mason simply wasn't ready to use it.

You should now understand:

- Why activity alone does not create stability or momentum in a real estate business
- How team environments and support systems shorten the learning curve without removing accountability
- That the recognition of what needs to change itself is the first act of professional growth
- Why "you finally want to hear it" matters — readiness determines whether information becomes action
- What shifts internally when an agent stops waiting for business and decides to build toward it with intention

* * *

CHAPTER 2

Small Habits Build Strong Roots

"Small habits become the roots of every strong business."

* * *

Elias motioned for Mason to sit.

"You're working hard," he said. "But you're missing the part that matters most."

Mason sat forward. "I'm listening."

Elias pulled out a worksheet. The title at the top was simple: *Warm Touchpoints.*

"This," Elias said, "is the most powerful habit in real estate. And you're not doing it."

Mason frowned. "I stay in touch with people."

Elias shook his head slowly.

"No. You follow up with leads. That's different."

He held up the sheet. "A warm touchpoint is simple. It's human. It's connection for connection's sake- not follow-up because you want something. Connection because you genuinely care. About the person. About their life. Not about whether they're buying or selling."

He listed examples on the whiteboard:

- Checking in on a past client's new neighborhood — how's the house settling?
- Sending a helpful article you genuinely thought they'd enjoy
- Congratulating someone on a job promotion or life update you saw on social media
- Asking how their family is doing — and meaning it
- Sharing local information, you know they'd appreciate
- Sending a quick voice memo or video message just to say hello

"It's not about real estate," Elias said. "It's about relationships. The real estate comes later. The relationship has to come first."

"How many?" Mason asked.

"Five a day," Elias said. "Every day. No excuses."

Mason blinked. "Just five?"

Elias leaned back. "Just five — consistently. Not ten one day and zero the next. Not bursts of effort followed by silence. Not a phone dump when you need business and then crickets when you're busy. Daily, predictable, steady."

He tapped the page.

"Most agents don't have a lead problem. They have a relationship problem. They treat their database like a place to call when they need money. By then it feels transactional. And people can sense that."

Mason looked at the worksheet again. Five a day. It sounded almost insultingly simple.

"What if it feels awkward?" he asked. "Like I'm performing instead of connecting?"

"It will," Elias said. "The first week, it will feel forced. That's normal. Push through it." He paused. "The awkwardness isn't a sign you're doing it wrong. It's a sign you're doing something new. The discomfort fades. The habit doesn't."

He leaned forward slightly.

"The other thing I'll tell you: start with the people who make you smile. Don't start with the lukewarm lead from eight months ago who never called you back. Start with people you genuinely like. Make the first few easy."

* * *

The next morning, Mason walked into the office early, coffee in hand, and opened his database.

He scanned the names — a hundred and forty-something contacts, most of them untouched for weeks. Some for months. A few from his first weeks of licensing who he'd essentially abandoned once the licensing exam excitement wore off.

Five warm touchpoints sounded easy yesterday.

Now, looking at the screen in the stillness of early morning, with the parking lot outside still half-empty and the coffee still too hot to drink, it felt strangely intimidating.

Elias passed by his desk on the way to the kitchen.

"Start with the people who make you smile," he said, without breaking stride.

So, Mason did.

He messaged a past buyer to ask how she was settling into the new neighborhood — had her son found friends at the elementary school? He sent a genuine congratulations to an old coworker whose promotion he'd seen online the week before and had been meaning to acknowledge. He called a former colleague just to catch up, no agenda, no pitch, fifteen minutes of conversation about life and the coast and whether the fishing had been any good this fall.

He sent a quick video message to a couple he'd shown homes to months ago, checking in and wishing them well on their search — wherever it had led. He'd always felt a little guilty about losing touch with them.

Four touches. He needed one more.

He thought about a woman he'd met at an open house nearly a year ago — she'd been curious, asked intelligent questions, and then gone quiet after two follow-up attempts. The professional thing he'd always assumed was to leave her alone. Not to be the agent who wouldn't take a hint.

Instead, he sent a short, genuine note: *Hey — I've been thinking about the conversation we had last spring. No agenda, just wanted to say I hope your plans are coming along well. If there's ever anything I can help with, I'm here.*

Five touches. Done in under twenty minutes.

And something surprising happened:

It felt good.

Not salesy. Not awkward. Not the uncomfortable performance he'd dreaded. Just human. Like waving at a neighbor or dropping a friend a note just because they crossed your mind.

He sat at his desk for a moment after finishing, slightly stunned by how simple it had been.

* * *

By the end of the week, five touches a day felt natural. By the end of two weeks, they were part of his morning routine — as automatic as checking his email, but more meaningful. He started the day with people, not tasks.

He didn't see dramatic results. No flood of referrals. No phones ringing off the hook. But he felt something different inside himself: a quiet sense of forward motion. The sense that he was tending something that would grow.

Two weeks in, he stopped by Charlotte's office.

She looked up from her laptop. "How's it going?"

"I'm doing the warm touches," Mason said. "Every day."

Charlotte raised an eyebrow. "And?"

"I think it's working," he said. "Not in giant ways. But I feel more connected. People respond. Conversations feel easier. Less transactional."

Charlotte smiled slowly.

"That's the point," she said. "A database is a garden, Mason. If you water it, it grows. If you ignore it, it dies. And the mistake most agents make is thinking a database that existed last year is still alive this year if they haven't touched it."

He nodded. "I'm starting to get it."

Charlotte leaned back in her chair.

"Good. Because your next step is ten warm touches a day."

Mason stared at her.

"Ten?"

"You're more capable than you think," she said. "And you're building the habits now that your future business will depend on. This isn't just a lead generation strategy. This is the culture of your business — who you are to the people in your life. That culture gets formed now, when it's easier to build it deliberately."

Ten a day felt like a lot.

But so had five — before he started.

He thought about Elias's words: *daily, predictable, steady.* He thought about the garden metaphor. You don't grow a garden by watering it hard once a week and ignoring it the rest of the time. You showed up every day, a little water, consistent light.

"I'll do it," Mason said.

"Of course you will," Charlotte replied. "You're ready for it."

* * *

What Mason was beginning to understand — slowly, through the simple act of showing up with his phone and a genuine curiosity about the people in his database — was something no training manual had ever captured for him.

Freedom requires discipline.

Not the rigid, joyless kind of discipline that squeezes spontaneity out of a day. The structural kind. The kind that creates the conditions where good things can happen repeatedly, not just occasionally.

Elias explained it in their first conversation: real estate is flexible by nature. Clients don't keep banker's hours. Markets don't respect your plans. But flexibility only works when it's supported by consistency. The freedom to work when you want only feels like freedom when you've already done the non-negotiable work. The spontaneous lunch with a client is a joy when you've already made your five calls. It's avoidance when it's all you did that day.

Mason had always thought structure and freedom were opposites. The license was supposed to give him freedom from a rigid schedule — from punching in and answering to someone else's clock.

Now he was beginning to understand they were partners.

The warm touches weren't a constraint.

They were roots.

And roots, he was learning, were what allowed everything else to stand upright — through calm stretches and storms alike.

* * *

FOUNDATION MARKER

Leadership Window: Freedom Is Sustained by Discipline

Flexibility without consistency eventually becomes chaos. The agents who build lasting businesses don't have less structure than everyone else — they have structure that's invisible because it's so deeply habitual. The daily warm touch isn't a task. It's the practice of staying human in a profession that can easily become transactional.

You should now understand:

- Why warm touchpoints are fundamentally different from lead follow-up — and why that distinction determines how they feel and how they land
- How to begin a daily touchpoint practice, including where to start and what to say when it feels awkward
- Why the discomfort of building a new consistent habit is a signal of growth, not a reason to stop
- How five daily touches compounds into ten, and then into a sustainable relationship culture that produces inbound referrals
- Why discipline — the non-glamorous kind — is the actual foundation of an agent's freedom

* * *

CHAPTER 3

Understanding Your Numbers Without Fear

"Awareness creates control. Numbers don't create pressure — avoiding them does."

* * *

Elias didn't start with leads.

He started with math.

"Before you grow," he told Mason the next morning, "you need to know what it costs you to exist."

Mason hesitated. "That sounds heavier than it is, right?"

Elias nodded. "Only until you put it on paper. Then it gets lighter."

He slid a worksheet across the desk — clean, simple, two columns.

"Burn rate is simple," Elias said. "It's just this:"

Monthly Burn Rate = Business Expenses + Personal Income Needs

"That's it. No mystery. No accounting degree required."

* * *

Together, they began listing numbers. Mason had never done this before — not formally, not completely. He'd operated by feel, by the approximate sense of whether things were going okay, by the relief of a closing or the ambient anxiety of a quiet week. He knew roughly what he owed and roughly what he earned, and for eight months he'd been betting that "roughly" was enough.

It wasn't.

Business expenses:

- MLS dues
- Brokerage and team fees
- CRM and tech tools
- Marketing and advertising
- Gas and vehicle costs

- Education and licensing
- Insurance and subscriptions

Then Elias added the second column.

Personal income needs:

- Rent
- Utilities
- Food
- Insurance
- Debt payments
- Savings target
- Anything Mason needed to exist without panic

They went through each line carefully. Mason knew some of the numbers off the top of his head. Others required a quick search through his banking app. A few he'd genuinely never thought about as business costs — the MLS subscription he paid every quarter, the E&O insurance deducted from his commission, the gas he'd been mentally filing as "just driving around."

They totaled the columns.

Mason stared at the final number.

"That's higher than I expected."

"That's normal," Elias replied, without alarm or judgment. "And it's not a failure. It's awareness."

He let the number sit there for a moment.

"This is your monthly burn rate. It's the minimum your business must produce each month before you're actually moving forward. Everything below this number is survival. You're paying to exist but not growing. Everything above it is margin — the breathing room where real momentum lives."

* * *

Elias continued.

"Now let's connect it to reality."

He pulled out a calculator.

"If your burn rate is $6,500 per month, and your average commission after splits and taxes is $8,000 per closing, here's what that means in plain language."

He wrote it out:

$6,500 ÷ $8,000 = 0.8 closings

"One closing covers your existence," Elias said. "It keeps the lights on. The second closing is where growth, margin, and breathing room begin."

Mason exhaled.

He hadn't expected it to feel like relief. He'd expected the numbers to make things worse — more visible, more frightening. Instead, something was loosening in his chest. The vague anxiety he'd been carrying about whether the business was "working" suddenly had a shape. A real shape, with specific edges.

"When agents don't know this number," Elias continued, "every closing feels dramatic. Relief one month. Panic the next. Not because the business is broken, but because the math is invisible. When the math is invisible, you can't tell the difference between a slow month that's normal and a slow month that's dangerous."

He leaned back.

"When you know your burn rate, you stop guessing. You stop reacting. You make decisions from facts instead of fear."

Mason looked at the page again.

Nothing about the number had changed. The expenses were the same. His income was the same. But everything about how he felt about them had shifted. The uncertainty was gone, replaced by something clearer: a minimum target, a concrete goal, a foundation for every decision about spending, pricing, and effort.

For the first time, he could see his business clearly.

Not emotionally.

Factually.

* * *

"Here's the next question," Elias said, pulling out a fresh sheet. "Once you know your burn rate, what does it tell you about your goals?"

Mason thought for a moment. "It tells me how many closings I actually need. Not to feel okay — but to actually move forward. To save money, grow, be strategic."

"Exactly." Elias leaned forward. "And here's where most agents make their first real strategic error: they set their targets based on fear of falling below their burn rate rather than ambition about exceeding it. They aim for survival and then wonder why the business always feels like it's just barely working."

He wrote two lines on the page:

Survival line: X closings per month — keeping the lights on

Growth line: X + 1 or 2 closings per month — margin, investment, momentum

"When you know the difference between those two lines, your behavior changes. You're not calling people out of desperation — you're executing a plan. Your pipeline has a destination. And clients can sense the difference between an agent who needs the deal and an agent who's working from a position of clarity."

Mason nodded slowly, processing.

"And it changes how I think about expenses too," he said. "If I want to run a Facebook ad or pay for a better CRM, I know exactly what return I need to justify it. The decision has a framework."

Elias pointed at him. "Now you're thinking like a business owner."

It was the first time anyone had said that to Mason.

Business owner.

Not agent. Not licensee.

The distinction landed somewhere important. An agent transacted. A business owner built a system that transacted reliably, month after month.

* * *

Before Mason left, Elias said something he would return to many times in the months ahead.

"Numbers don't create pressure, Mason. Avoiding them does. When the math is invisible, every slow week feels existential — like evidence that maybe this business doesn't work for you. When the math is clear, a slow week is just a slow week. You know what caused it, you know what to adjust, and you keep going."

He paused.

"Fear lives in the unknown. Clarity is its antidote."

Mason folded the worksheet and slipped it into his notebook.

He didn't have a perfect business yet. He didn't have a full pipeline yet. He didn't even have his ten warm touches fully dialed in.

But he had his number.

And for the first time, he knew exactly what the ground beneath him looked like.

And that — that clarity — felt steady in a way nothing in the past eight months had.

* * *

On the walk back to his car, Mason thought about the agents he knew who'd been in the business for years and still felt anxious between closings. He'd always assumed it was because real estate was inherently unpredictable — that the income swings were just the price of the work. Now he wondered if it was something simpler. If the anxiety wasn't about the market at all. If it was about the invisible math.

How many of them knew their burn rate? How many had ever calculated, precisely, what it cost them to exist each month? How many could tell you, without hesitation, how many closings stood between them and genuine financial breathing room?

He guessed the number was small.

And he understood now why. Looking at the math was uncomfortable. It required confronting the gap between what you thought you earned and what you actually needed. It required admitting that the business you were building had real costs, real risks, and real requirements — not just aspirations.

But once you looked, the discomfort dissolved. What was left was information. And information, Mason was learning, was the raw material of every good decision.

He sat in his car for a moment before starting the engine.

He still had the same burn rate. The same pipeline. The same work ahead of him.

But now he knew exactly where he stood.

And that made all the difference.

* * *

FOUNDATION MARKER

Leadership Window: Awareness Creates Control

Numbers don't create pressure — avoiding them does. When an agent knows their burn rate, slow weeks become data points rather than emotional crises. Financial clarity isn't a bookkeeping exercise. It is a form of professional confidence — the difference between operating from fear and operating from facts.

You should now understand:

- How to calculate your monthly burn rate using the simple formula: Business Expenses + Personal Income Needs
- Why the burn rate is your true starting line each month — not an arbitrary wish, but the minimum required for forward movement
- How to connect your burn rate to specific closing targets so daily activity has a clear destination
- Why financial visibility reduces anxiety rather than amplifying it — and why most agents feel relief when they finally do the math
- The difference between the survival line and the growth line, and why that gap is where a business is actually built

* * *

CHAPTER 4

Where the Commission Actually Goes

"Profit is a system, not a bonus. If it only happens when things go well, it's not a system — it's luck."

* * *

Mason thought he understood commissions.

He knew what he earned on paper. What he didn't understand was why money still felt tight even after a "good" closing. Why the relief of a commission check never lasted as long as it should. Why, by the following month, he was back in the same familiar cycle of hoping the next one would come before the last one ran out.

Elias fixed that in one meeting.

"Most agents fail financially not because they don't earn enough," he said, settling into his chair, "but because they don't tell their money what to do."

He pulled out a clean sheet of paper.

"Before we talk about saving, profit, or paying yourself consistently, you need to understand how money actually moves through your business. The path it takes before it ever becomes income."

Mason leaned in.

* * *

How a Commission Is Actually Broken Down

Elias started with a concrete example.

"Let's say you represent the buyer on a sale and earn a $10,000 gross commission. That's the number in the contract. Here's what happens to it before it lands anywhere useful."

He wrote as he spoke.

Franchise fee (off the top): If the brokerage is part of a national franchise — and most are — a percentage is deducted from the gross commission before anything else is calculated. You often don't see this line. It happens quietly, at the brokerage level, before your split is even calculated.

Brokerage split: The brokerage takes its agreed share of what remains. This varies by agreement and market, but it's always real money — sometimes significant money.

Team split: If you're on a team, the remaining amount is then split according to your team compensation agreement.

Elias underlined the final number.

"What lands in your business account," he said, "is not your paycheck. It's revenue."

The distinction landed harder than Mason expected.

"Revenue," he repeated.

"Not income. Revenue is what the business receives. Income is what you eventually keep after running the business. Those are not the same number and treating them as if they are is one of the most common and costly mistakes in this industry."

Elias continued. "This is where most agents get into trouble. They see a commission check and experience something like psychological relief. The money arrived, therefore they're okay. And then they spend it — because it feels like their paycheck — before it ever has a job to do."

Mason thought about every closing he'd had. The exhale. The loosening of tension. The quiet sense of *okay, I'm fine* — that would last until the next slow stretch.

"So, I've been doing that," he said.

"Almost every agent does, early on," Elias replied. "It's not a character flaw. It's a missing piece of financial education that nobody gives you when you get your license."

* * *

Understanding a Profit & Loss Statement

Elias slid another page across the desk.

"This is where a Profit & Loss statement comes in. A P&L is simply a snapshot that shows where your money came from and where it went during a specific period — usually monthly or annually."

He broke it down.

Revenue: Total commissions deposited into the business account after splits.

Expenses: Everything it costs to run the business. Brokerage and team fees. Marketing and advertising. Technology and CRM subscriptions. MLS dues. Gas and vehicle costs. Education, conferences, and professional development. Anything spent operating the business.

Net Profit (or Loss): What remains after all expenses are subtracted from revenue.

Elias walked Mason through a concrete example.

"Let's say you bring in $120,000 in commissions this year. That's your revenue — the money that actually reaches your business account after splits. Then you spend $100,000 running the business: brokerage fees, marketing, gas, MLS dues, CRM subscriptions, advertising, that conference in the fall. Your P&L subtracts expenses from revenue, leaving $20,000 as net profit."

Mason frowned, staring at the numbers. "Okay. But I've had months where I earned real commissions and didn't feel like I made anything. The money landed and then it was just... gone. I still felt squeezed."

"Exactly," Elias said, leaning forward. "That's the disconnect. Profit on paper doesn't automatically become profit in your life. Your P&L shows what the business earned. It doesn't tell that money where to go next. It sits in your business account — or your personal account, if you haven't separated them yet — mixing with this month's expenses, until you spend it. Or until you forget it's there and something else takes it."

He tapped the page firmly.

"A P&L tells the truth about what happened last month. But it doesn't enforce behavior for what happens next. There's no guardrail that says 'set aside 30% for taxes right now' or 'pay yourself a consistent draw before touching the rest.' Without that next step, even a technically profitable business feels like it's always one slow month from stress. Because it is."

Mason sat with that for a moment. He'd been treating business revenue like personal income — reacting to what landed in the account rather than directing it with intention. The P&L wasn't the problem. The problem was the gap between where the money appeared and where it needed to go.

* * *

Introducing Profit First Thinking

Elias leaned back. "Now let's talk about what most agents never do."

He wrote four simple categories on the page:

Profit
Owner Pay
Taxes
Operating Expenses

"Most businesses operate like this," Elias said. "Money comes in. Bills get paid. Whatever's left goes into savings — if anything's left. This is called 'pay expenses first and hope there's something remaining.'"

He paused. "Profit First flips that entirely. Instead of paying expenses first and hoping there's something left, you allocate intentionally. You decide what matters before you spend a dollar."

"Even starting with 1% profit changes everything," he added.

Mason raised an eyebrow. "One percent?"

"Yes," Elias said. "Because profit isn't about the amount. It's about the habit. The discipline of setting aside something for profit — even a token amount at first — breaks the psychological loop of 'there's never anything left.' It proves to yourself and to the business that profit is something you create on purpose, not something that appears accidentally."

He walked through each category.

Profit: A small percentage set aside first. Not as a reward when things go well — as proof the business is healthy. It starts small and grows as the business grows. This is the money that proves you're running a real business, not just a self-employed job.

Owner Pay: Your actual paycheck. Predictable. Stable. Not "whatever's left at the end of the month" a planned, consistent draw that you can build a life around.

Taxes: Set aside consistently after every commission, not stockpiled in a panic before April. The number that gets agents in trouble isn't the tax bill itself — it's the surprise of it arriving without any preparation.

Operating Expenses: What's left is what the business is allowed to spend on operations. The model keeps expenses honest because expenses don't expand infinitely into whatever revenue is available.

He sketched out an example:

> Revenue: $10,000 commission → > > Profit — 10% ($1,000) →separate profit account > > Owner Pay — 50% ($5,000) → personal account > > Taxes — 30% ($3,000) → tax account > > Operating Expenses — 10% ($1,000) → business spending

"These percentages are illustrative," Elias said. "Every business is different. The percentages shift as income grows. But the concept is the point: allocate first. Build the habit of directing money before it disappears into the chaos of daily expenses."

Mason thought about the past year. The stress between closings. The constant feeling of catching up — of working toward something that kept slipping just out of reach.

"So, I don't wait to see what's left at the end of the month?"

"No," Elias replied. "You decide in advance what matters, and you make sure those decisions happen every time money comes in, not once a year when you're trying to figure out where it all went."

For the first time, Mason understood something that felt genuinely new.

Financial stability wasn't about more closings.

It was about telling the money where to go before it had the chance to disappear.

He walked out of Elias's office that afternoon with two pages of notes and a clarity he hadn't felt in months.

The numbers weren't the enemy. They'd never been the enemy.

The invisible numbers — the unexamined, untracked, unplanned flow of money through his life and his business — that was the enemy. That was what had been creating the low-grade financial anxiety that sat underneath everything.

Now he could see the whole picture.

And a picture you can see is a picture you can change.

* * *

FOUNDATION MARKER

Leadership Window: Profit Is a System, Not a Bonus

If profit only happens when things go well, it's not a system — it's luck. Allocating profit intentionally, even a small percentage at first, is what separates agents who build wealth from agents who generate income and wonder where it went. The amount matters far less than the habit of protecting it.

You should now understand:

- How a commission is broken down step by step — from gross commission to what actually reaches your account
- The critical difference between revenue and income, and why confusing them leads to the most common financial stress in real estate
- How to read a basic Profit & Loss statement and what it tells you about business health
- Why profit on paper doesn't automatically become financial security without intentional allocation
- How Profit First principles work in a real estate context — and why even 1% is enough to start building the right habits

* * *

CHAPTER 5

Your CRM Is a Living System

"Systems only work when they're used completely. Partial systems create false confidence."

* * *

Two weeks after his financial conversations with Elias, Mason heard a knock at his door.

Maya Ellis was the team's Client Care Coordinator, and she moved through the office with the focused efficiency of someone who always had a next step in mind. Her role was the full arc of the client experience — from the moment a contract was signed through years after the keys were handed over. She made sure no client ever felt forgotten, no deadline ever crept up unannounced, no follow-up ever fell through the floor.

She managed contract-to-close coordination with quiet precision: documents, deadlines, communication threads between agents, lenders, attorneys, and inspectors. Timeline boards. Addendums drafted before they were needed. Extension requests filed before anyone had to ask. She was the infrastructure that kept transactions moving between the signed agreement and the closing table, the kind of work that was invisible when it was done well and catastrophic when it wasn't.

But client care extended well beyond the closing table.

Maya owned the relationship after the sale. Post-closing follow-up. Annual check-ins. Long-term relationship tracking for past clients who might list again in two years or refer a family member next spring. Her job wasn't just to get clients to the finish line. It was to make sure they stayed connected to the team long after the keys were handed over.

She sat down beside Mason and turned her screen so he could see.

"Your CRM isn't full," she said gently. "It's unfinished."

She clicked into a contact — a couple Mason had shown homes to three months ago.

"No next task," she said, pointing to the empty task field. "That's how people get lost."

Mason leaned closer to the screen.

"This isn't about how many names you have in here," she continued. "It's about whether your database knows what's supposed to happen next with each one. Every contact must have a next action assigned. Every single one."

She paused, and her voice took on the particular tone of someone who'd watched this problem cause real harm.

"If there's no next task, the relationship goes dormant. Not because you stopped caring. But because the system doesn't know what to do, so it does nothing."

* * *

She demonstrated as she spoke, moving through the contact screen with practiced ease.

A call scheduled. A follow-up task set with a date. A note logged: *Moving in June. Has two dogs. Works in healthcare.*

Click. Click. Click.

"When your CRM is working properly," Maya explained, "it tells you exactly what to do each day. You're not relying on memory. You're not hoping you'll remember that somebody mentioned they were thinking of selling next fall. You're following a plan your past self built, so your present self doesn't have to hold everything in his head."

That was the missing piece Mason hadn't been able to name.

He'd been collecting contacts without direction. People weren't falling through the cracks because he didn't care — they were falling through because nothing was holding them in place. No task. No thread. No structured reason to reach back out.

"Your CRM should be the hub of your business," Maya said. "Every relationship, every transaction, every follow-up starts and lives here. Not in your phone's notes app. Not on a sticky note. Here — where you can see it, sequence it, and act on it."

She showed him how the team used the system.

Transaction stages: A clear, visible marker for exactly where each client was in the process. Not a vague sense of "I think they're still looking", a defined stage that told Mason what kind of engagement was appropriate.

Tags: Tools for sorting, segmenting, and finding the right people at the right moment. Buyers at different price points. Past clients by closing year. Sphere contacts by relationship type.

Tasks: The engine of the whole system. Every contact, a next action. Every next action, a date.

"When you're database-centric," she said, "your system carries the remembering. Your brain gets to focus on the actual work — the conversations, the negotiations, the human moments. You're not burning mental energy trying to remember who you were supposed to call last Thursday."

Mason felt the shift immediately.

The CRM wasn't another thing to manage. It was a structure that removed mental clutter. The difference between trying to hold a hundred conversations in his head and opening a list that told him exactly who needed what, today.

* * *

He started that afternoon.

Contact by contact, he went through his database. He added notes from memory. He assigned tasks. He gave every dormant record a next step — some of them immediately, some of them scheduled months out.

It took three days to work through the full list.

But something changed as he went. He started noticing things he'd forgotten. A buyer who'd gone quiet in the spring — she'd mentioned her lease ending in December. He added a task: *Call in November. Ask how the search is going.* A past client who'd asked about the investment property market last summer — he'd never followed up. He added a note and scheduled a call.

And then Elias stopped by his desk one afternoon and showed him the next layer.

"You're doing the CRM right," Elias said, looking over his shoulder. "Here's what takes it further." He pointed to a contact named Ethan — one of Mason's active buyers. "What do you know about him outside the transaction?"

Mason shrugged. "He and Claire are first-time buyers. Moving from Raleigh. Have a dog named Briar."

"Good. Write it down. All of it." Elias leaned back. "Now — when's their wedding anniversary? Does he follow sports? Does Claire have a birthday coming up?"

Mason blinked. "I... don't know most of that."

"Find out," Elias said. "Not in an interrogation — in the natural course of conversation. And when you learn it, log it. Because your CRM is not a contact list."

He paused and let the next sentence land.

"You're not building a contact list. You're building a relationship map."

Mason liked that immediately. A map felt like something navigable. Something that had a logic to it, a structure, a way of showing you not just where people were but how to get to them.

* * *

A few weeks later, he was walking Ethan and Claire through a showing when Claire mentioned offhand that their move date was tied to a family event — her nephew's high school graduation.

Old Mason would have nodded and moved on.

New Mason said, "When's the graduation? Let's make sure your closing timeline doesn't create any stress around that week."

Claire stopped walking and looked at him.

"You're thinking about that?"

"I have it in my notes," Mason said honestly. "You mentioned it when we first talked about timing."

She laughed softly. "Most people would have said 'congrats' and forgotten about it. I appreciate that."

He went back to the office that afternoon and logged the detail. Added a task to send a card around the graduation date. Nothing elaborate. Just a small, specific acknowledgment that he'd been paying attention.

Small. Specific. Human.

That was what the CRM was for. Not data for data's sake. Relationship memory — organized, searchable, and actionable — so Mason could show up to every conversation as someone who paid attention and remembered what mattered.

He was beginning to understand something important: the problem had never been the size of his database. It was the lack of direction inside it.

A full CRM with no tasks was just a list.

A full CRM with every contact anchored to a next step was a system.

And systems, as Elias had said, don't burn out.

* * *

That evening, Mason sat at his kitchen table with his laptop open and his CRM on the screen.

He went through twenty more contacts — not because Maya had told him to, not because there was a deadline, but because it felt productive in a way that pure activity never had. Adding a note about someone's upcoming move. Scheduling a call for someone who'd mentioned an anniversary coming up. Writing down that a past client's son was heading to college in the fall — a detail worth remembering, worth acknowledging when the time came.

Each entry took two or three minutes. Together they took less than an hour.

But when he closed the laptop, he felt something that had been absent for most of the past year: the quiet confidence of someone who knows who they're supposed to call tomorrow, and the day after, and the week after that. No scrambling. No guessing. No sinking feeling that important people were quietly drifting out of reach.

The database knew what to do.

And because the database knew, Mason could stop carrying it all in his head.

He thought about what Maya had said — *partial systems create false confidence.* He'd had a CRM for eight months and believed he was being organized. He'd been entering names and doing nothing with them. The system existed on paper. It hadn't been alive.

Now it was.

And the difference wasn't a feature he'd discovered or a tool he'd upgraded. It was a discipline: every contact, every task, every note. Used completely. Trusted completely. Followed through.

He closed his laptop and went to bed feeling, for the first time in months, like he knew exactly who he was in this business.

He was the agent who remembered.

* * *

FOUNDATION MARKER

Leadership Window: Systems Only Work When They're Used Completely

Partial systems create false confidence. An agent who enters contacts but never assigns next tasks believes they have a working CRM when they actually have a storage file. The system's entire value is in its follow-through — every contact, every task, every note. Used completely, a CRM doesn't just organize people. It makes genuine relationships possible at scale.

You should now understand:

- Why every contact must have a next task assigned — and what happens to relationships when they don't
- The difference between a contact list and a relationship map, and why only one of them produces consistent referrals
- How a well-maintained CRM eliminates the mental burden of remembering who you need to call, and replaces anxiety with a clear daily plan
- Why client care extends well beyond the closing table — and how that long-term focus compounds over years
- How small personal details, logged and acted on, create the kind of attentiveness that makes clients feel genuinely cared for rather than managed

* * *

CHAPTER 6

Asking for Referrals Without Being Salesy

"Confidence removes pressure. When your service is solid, the ask feels natural."

* * *

Mason hated asking for referrals.

Not mildly disliked. Genuinely dreaded.

Every time the thought surfaced, he felt something clench in his chest — the anticipatory discomfort of doing something that felt transactional and desperate. Like he was reaching into a relationship and pulling something out of it. Like he was the agent who had been nice to someone for months just to eventually pitch them.

He knew intellectually that referrals were the lifeblood of a sustainable real estate business. He'd heard that truth in training sessions, in podcasts, in conversations with more experienced agents. But knowing it and doing it were two entirely different things.

And so, he didn't ask. He waited. He hoped. He told himself that if he just kept doing good work, the referrals would come naturally.

Sometimes they did.

More often, they didn't — not because people wouldn't have referred him, but because the idea of Mason as *their real estate agent* simply never surfaced at the right moment. He was present enough to be liked. He wasn't present enough to be top of mind.

Charlotte noticed the hesitation during one of their regular check-ins.

"You're not asking for referrals," she said. It wasn't a question.

Mason shifted in his chair. "It feels like I'm asking people to do me a favor."

Charlotte leaned forward.

"You're not asking for business," she said. "You're inviting trust."

She let that distinction sit in the room for a moment.

"Here's what you're getting wrong: you think asking for referrals is about you. It isn't. It's about giving someone who already trusts you the opportunity to help someone they care about. You're not extracting something from the relationship. You're extending it. You're giving your best clients the chance to do something genuinely useful for the people in their lives."

Mason sat with that.

"That's a completely different frame," he said.

"Yes," Charlotte said. "And it changes everything about how you say it."

* * *

Two months into his warm touchpoint practice, he now building toward ten a day — Mason ran into Susan at a coffee shop near the waterfront.

She'd bought her home with him months earlier. The transaction had gone smoothly. The follow-up had been genuine and consistent — not salesy, just present. They'd exchanged messages about the neighborhood, about her dog settling in, about the storm that had knocked a branch through her fence and how she'd used the vendor list Elias maintained to find a contractor quickly.

The system had worked quietly, invisibly. She felt taken care of. She remembered Mason not because he'd been aggressive about follow-up, but because the follow-up had been thoughtful.

They chatted for a few minutes — about work, about the waterfront, about the way the town softened in spring before the tourists arrived.

As they wrapped up, Mason felt the familiar hesitation rise in his chest.

Don't ask. It'll seem like that's why you said hello.

Then he remembered Charlotte's words.

He didn't rush. He didn't pitch.

He simply said: "I really enjoyed working with you last year. I try to build my business through people I already know and serve well. If you ever hear someone talking about buying or selling, I'd be honored if you'd think of me."

She didn't hesitate.

"Oh, absolutely," she said. "Actually — my neighbor just mentioned they might be relocating this spring. I didn't even think about it until right now."

Mason smiled. "If it makes sense, I'm always happy to help. No pressure."

"I'll connect you," she said easily. "You made the whole process so calm for us. I'd feel good sending someone your way."

That was it.

No pitch. No discomfort. No awkward pause.

Just a natural, human moment — the kind that only happened because the foundation underneath it had been built, patiently, over months.

* * *

Later, Mason told Charlotte about the coffee shop.

She nodded slowly, satisfied.

"See? When your service is solid, the ask feels natural. Because you weren't asking for a favor. You were reminding her that you exist and telling her she has an opportunity to help someone she cares about. Those are two very different things."

She reminded him of the language she'd given him — simple, human, pressure-free. Language that opened doors rather than applying pressure.

"Here are a few ways to phrase it," Charlotte said.

"If you know anyone who could use the same level of care I gave you, I'd be honored to help them."

"I build my business through people I already know and serve well. If someone comes to mind, feel free to connect us."

"I never expect referrals, but I always appreciate introductions."

"None of those are scripts," she said. "They're stances. A way of presenting yourself that's confident but not pushy. What you're communicating is: I'm good at this, I'm not desperate, and I'd welcome the opportunity. That's very different from 'do you know anyone who needs a real estate agent?' which sounds like you're running out of options."

Mason thought about his old approach — the hopeful waiting, the resigned silence, the deals he'd probably lost simply because he'd never given people a clear, comfortable way to send him business.

"I've been thinking about this all wrong," he said.

"Most agents do," Charlotte replied. "They treat referrals like a withdrawal from a relationship account. If you've been making regular deposits — genuine care, consistent follow-up, real service — then asking isn't a withdrawal. It's just acknowledging that the account exists."

* * *

Within weeks, Mason noticed something he hadn't experienced before.

The warm touches were compounding. People he hadn't heard from in months were responding. A past client asked for a market analysis on her neighborhood — thinking about the equity she'd built. A former colleague's cousin mentioned buying after the new year. A vendor partner sent him a name, unprompted.

None of it was dramatic.

But the accumulation was unmistakable.

He walked past Charlotte's office one afternoon, and she called out without looking up.

"Told you."

"Told me what?" he asked.

"That consistency compounds," she said. "Quietly at first. Then suddenly."

He thought about the coffee shop. About Susan. About the way the referral conversation had felt nothing like what he'd always feared — not transactional, not desperate, just a natural extension of a relationship that had been built with care.

He was starting to understand something important: asking for referrals wasn't about extracting something. It was about standing confidently in the value of what he did — and giving the people who already believed in that value a clear way to share it.

That confidence was something you earned.

One warm touch at a time. One genuine conversation at a time. One closing that went smoothly because the whole system underneath it was working.

* * *

Mason thought, on the drive back to the office, about all the agents he'd heard complain about referrals.

People don't think of me. My sphere keeps using other agents. I do great work, but nobody sends me business.

He'd said versions of all of those things himself.

But sitting with it now, he understood something different. The problem hadn't been the people in his database. They were perfectly willing to refer him — once the idea surfaced, once a connection formed between their friend's need and Mason's name.

The problem was that he'd never given them a clear way in. He'd never made the ask comfortable. He'd never positioned it as a gift rather than a transaction.

Charlotte had said it plainly: *you're not asking for business. You're inviting trust.*

And the invitation he was learning only worked when the groundwork had been laid. When the calls had been made. When the follow-ups had been consistent. When the client's experience had been genuinely good and the post-closing relationship had been maintained with real care.

The referral conversation wasn't the work.

It was the harvest.

The work was everything that came before it — the warm touches, the CRM discipline, the service that made people feel seen and remembered rather than processed.

Done in that order, the ask was easy.

Done out of that order, it would always feel like a transaction.

Mason pulled into the parking lot, already thinking about which past clients he wanted to reach out to this week — not to ask for anything, just to stay present. To water the garden, as Charlotte had said.

The referrals would come.

They were already starting to.

* * *

FOUNDATION MARKER

Leadership Window: Confidence Removes Pressure

When your service is solid, asking feels natural — because you're not asking for a favor. You're giving someone who already trusts you the chance to help someone they care about. The referral conversation, done with confidence and genuine care, is an act of service to both parties. The discipline that makes this possible isn't the referral ask itself. It's everything that came before it.

You should now understand:

- How to reframe referral conversations as an invitation to help rather than a request for personal business
- Why consistent service creates the conditions that make referrals feel natural rather than awkward
- Specific language for asking for referrals without pressure — and why the phrasing reflects a stance, not a script
- How warm touchpoints compound over weeks and months into inbound connections — people reaching out to you without being asked
- Why the shift from chasing business to receiving it is a direct, predictable result of disciplined relationship-building

* * *

CHAPTER 7

Time Is the First System

"Your calendar should reflect your goals, not your stress."

* * *

Mason didn't come back to Charlotte because something had gone wrong.

He came back because something had started working — and he needed help holding it.

His days were fuller now. More conversations. More follow-up. More activity in his pipeline than he'd had in his first eight months combined. He'd closed two transactions in the past six weeks and had two more in motion. His warm touches had become a genuine morning ritual. The CRM was alive in a way it had never been before.

And yet, by mid-afternoon most days, he still felt stretched thin. Like he was always reacting instead of leading his time. Like the hours were running him instead of the other way around.

He knew things he hadn't known before. He had his burn rate. He had his CRM. He had his five-daily-touch habit — working toward ten. He had more to show for his efforts than at any point in the past year.

But something wasn't finished.

He knocked lightly on Charlotte's open door.

"I think I need help again," he said.

She smiled. "That's usually a good sign."

They sat across from each other. Only this time, Mason wasn't overwhelmed by chaos. He was overwhelmed by choices.

"I feel busy all day," he admitted. "But I'm not always sure I'm doing the right things. I finish a day and I can't always tell you what I actually accomplished."

Charlotte didn't sugarcoat it.

"You don't have a time problem," she said. "You have a decision problem."

She leaned back. "When there's no system for deciding what matters, the loudest thing wins. And the loudest thing is almost never the most important thing."

She paused.

"Urgency feels productive. It's also a trap."

* * *

Charlotte introduced three tools that changed how Mason worked almost immediately:

- Daily routines
- Weekly time blocks
- Priority filtering

Then she stood, picked up a marker, and walked to the whiteboard.

"Let me show you how to see your time clearly."

She drew a simple four-quadrant box.

"Everything you do fits somewhere in this matrix," she said. "The goal isn't to eliminate urgency. It's to contain it — so it doesn't consume everything else."

* * *

Quadrant 1: Do Now — Urgent and Important

Charlotte tapped the upper-left box.

"Deal protectors. These get handled immediately — not because they're loud, but because they matter."

Real estate examples: offer deadlines, inspection issues, appraisal problems, a hot buyer ready to write, active negotiation calls.

"But Q1 should be temporary," she said. "If you live here permanently, you're always reacting. You'll burn out. And the work that actually grows your business will never get done."

She looked at Mason steadily.

"The tragedy isn't that Q1 exists. The tragedy is when it becomes the only place you operate."

* * *

Quadrant 2: Schedule — Important, Not Urgent

Charlotte tapped the upper-right box.

"This," she said, "is where businesses are built."

She let that sentence stand alone.

Real estate examples: lead generation, sphere follow-up, CRM maintenance, market analysis, client event planning.

"These go on your calendar. If you don't schedule them, they disappear — not because you forgot they mattered, but because Q1 will always crowd them out. The crisis always feels more urgent than the strategy."

She looked at Mason steadily.

"Top producers spend most of their time here. Not because they're less busy. Because they're more intentional. They've made peace with the fact that the important work rarely announces itself as loudly as the urgent work."

* * *

Quadrant 3: Delegate — Urgent, Not Important

"These feel pressing," Charlotte said, "but they don't require you specifically."

Real estate examples: transaction coordination, listing coordination, social media scheduling, vendor management.

"This is where your operations staff or systems step in. Urgent doesn't mean it's your job. And 'not important' doesn't mean it's not important to do — it means it's not important that *you* do it. Your highest-value contribution is relationship and negotiation. Everything else is a candidate for delegation."

Mason nodded. That distinction mattered. He'd been spending hours on things that needed doing but didn't need him specifically.

* * *

Quadrant 4: Review — Not Urgent, Not Important

"These drain time quietly," Charlotte said.

Real estate examples: endless home searches with no criteria, tire-kickers without commitment, office distraction, busywork disguised as productivity.

"These aren't evil," she added. "But unmanaged, they steal your best hours. And unlike Q1, they don't even feel important while they're happening. They just feel comfortable. A way to feel occupied without doing the hard work."

* * *

Charlotte capped the marker and brought it together.

"The Pareto Principle tells us that roughly 20% of your actions create 80% of your results."

In real estate, those actions were almost always: meaningful conversations, genuine follow-up, relationship deepening, and high-stakes negotiation.

"Time blocking protects those actions from being crowded out by everything else," she said.

She looked Mason in the eye.

"You don't find time for what matters. You decide first — then protect it. Those are different things. Finding implies it was hiding. Protecting implies you chose it."

* * *

That afternoon, Mason walked to the operations office.

Elias was already waiting.

"Charlotte called ahead," he said with a small smile. "Said you were ready to build your ideal week."

Mason laughed and sat down.

They spread out his current schedule — such as it was — and examined it together. What Mason saw when he looked at it clearly was both obvious and uncomfortable: there were no protected blocks. Every part of his day was available to whoever had the most urgent need at that moment. The person who called first, who texted most urgently, who had the deadline closest — they owned his time.

"The structure is missing," Elias said simply. "Right now, you have a schedule that happens to you. Let's build one that you happen to."

They reviewed four categories and placed every activity Mason did into one of them: Lead Generation, Lead Conversion, Client Service, Business Operations.

Then they built a structure.

Warm Touchpoints: Monday through Friday, 8:30 to 9:30 a.m. Non-negotiable. First hour of the day, before anything else.

Showings and Client Calls: Late mornings and afternoons, when clients were available and Mason had already done his proactive morning work.

Transaction Follow-Up: Tuesday and Thursday afternoons — a dedicated block for checking in on active deals without letting them bleed into everything else.

Financial Review and Operations: Thursday mornings, protected and brief. Ten minutes reviewing his numbers and updating his pipeline.

Protected Personal Time: Built into the structure by design — not squeezed in around the edges of everything else.

Mason stared at the finished grid.

"I feel calmer just looking at this."

"That's the point," Elias said. "A controlled schedule creates a controlled business. When you don't have a structure, every new task is a potential derailment. When you have a structure, every new task has a place to go — and you don't have to decide where that is in the moment."

* * *

Later that week, Charlotte sat with Mason one more time.

"You've made a lot of progress," she said. "Now there's one more piece. You need to know exactly where you're going. Vague goals produce vague results."

She slid a clean sheet of paper across the desk.

"Write this down."

He picked up his pen.

"Thirty-six units," she said. "A hundred thousand dollars net. Ten warm touches a day. One major client event. A scalable business." She paused. "And a calm mind."

Mason stared at the list.

"You think I can do this?"

Charlotte smiled.

"You wouldn't still be in this office if I didn't."

He thought about eight months ago — the full calendar that produced no momentum, the closings that brought relief followed immediately by anxiety, the feeling of running hard in every direction at once.

He thought about his burn rate, written on a worksheet in Elias's clear handwriting. About the warm touches that had started to compound. About Susan at the coffee shop, and the referral conversation that had felt so unexpectedly easy. About his CRM, now alive with next tasks and notes and the small personal details that made relationships feel real.

He looked at the goals on the page.

36 units. $100,000 net. Ten warm touches a day.

For the first time in eight months, he didn't feel like he was guessing.

He believed her.

* * *

FOUNDATION MARKER

Leadership Window: Time Reveals Priorities

Your calendar tells the truth before your words do. The agent who says relationships are their priority but schedules prospecting in the margins is showing you their real priority. Time blocking is not a scheduling trick — it is the physical expression of what you value. What gets protected gets done. What doesn't, doesn't.

You should now understand:

- How to use the Eisenhower Matrix to categorize every task in your real estate business by urgency and importance
- Why living permanently in Quadrant 1 (Urgent + Important) leads to burnout, stunted growth, and the constant feeling of falling behind
- Where real estate businesses are actually built — in Quadrant 2, the important-but-not-urgent work that never announces itself as urgent
- How time blocking protects high-value activities from being perpetually crowded out by immediate demands
- How to build an ideal week with clear, defended blocks for lead generation, client service, operations, and personal time
- Why specific annual goals (36 units, $100K net, 10 warm touches per day) are essential — vague ambitions produce vague results

* * *

FOUNDATION IN PRACTICE — PART I

Pouring the Foundation

* * *

Mason drove home along the coast road with the windows down.

It was early evening, and the marsh grass caught the gold of the lowering sun. On the right, the sound stretched flat and still toward the barrier islands, and a heron stood motionless in the shallows, unhurried and precise in the way only birds that hunt patiently ever are.

Six weeks.

He'd been at this for about six weeks — the warm touches, the burn rate, the CRM overhaul, the time blocking, the referral conversations, the financial frameworks Elias had walked him through with such patient clarity. Six weeks of the kind of slow, foundational work that didn't show up on anyone's highlight reel. No dramatic announcements. No viral posts. No impressive GCI screenshot.

Just the daily practice of building something that might actually hold.

And yet something had shifted.

He couldn't point to a single moment when it happened. It had come the way tides came in so gradually that you only noticed when you looked up and realized the water was somewhere entirely different than it had been.

* * *

He wasn't reacting the way he used to.

When a client went quiet, he didn't feel the familiar lurch of panic — he checked the CRM, saw when the next task was scheduled, and trusted the system to tell him what to do next. When a slow morning arrived, he didn't spiral — he opened his warm touchpoint list and started with the people who made him smile. When he looked at his numbers, the old vague anxiety was replaced by something closer to clarity: the burn rate in his notebook, a compass bearing that let him make decisions from facts rather than fear.

The chaos hadn't disappeared. Deals still got complicated. Clients still needed reassurance at unexpected hours. Life still interrupted plans. He'd had an inspection go sideways just last week and spent an afternoon managing everyone's emotions — including his own.

But for the first time, the chaos had somewhere to land.

It didn't derail him anymore. It just became the next task within a structure that was, slowly, unmistakably, holding.

* * *

He thought about Charlotte's office — the morning she'd said, *you're consistent at being inconsistent.* The words had stung, but only because they were exactly right. He'd been performing the motions of a business without building the bones.

He thought about Elias, patient and methodical, who had shown him that structure wasn't the opposite of freedom — it was the precondition for it. That your calendar didn't have to reflect your stress. That it could, if you chose intentionally, reflect your goals instead.

He thought about Maya and the CRM, and the simple revelation that a database without next tasks wasn't a system — it was storage. He thought about Susan at the coffee shop, and the referral that had arrived so naturally because the relationship underneath it had been tended so genuinely.

He thought about the burn rate sitting in his notebook. About the Profit First percentages on a sticky note on his monitor. About the time blocks on his calendar that he was already learning to protect like something precious.

He wasn't the same agent he'd been six weeks ago.

He wasn't finished — he knew that clearly. There was more to learn, more to build, more ways the foundation would be tested before it could be fully trusted. But something fundamental had changed.

He'd stopped waiting for the business to find him.

He'd started building the structure that the business could find.

* * *

Every contact in his CRM had a next task.

His calendar had protected blocks he actually defended.

His burn rate was a fixed star in a sky that used to feel entirely unpredictable.

His warm touches had become a reflex — a daily practice already starting to send quiet ripples back toward him in the form of conversations renewed, referrals surfacing, past clients remembering he existed.

Nothing about what he'd built in six weeks was glamorous. It wasn't the part of real estate that got written about or celebrated. It was the concrete work — the part below ground, invisible to everyone but essential to everything.

It was also, he was beginning to understand, the part that made everything else possible.

Systems turn effort into momentum.

Mason pulled into his parking spot, turned off the engine, and sat with that for a moment.

He used to think momentum was something that happened to you — a streak of luck, a hot market, a wave you caught or missed. Something external. Something granted.

Now he understood; momentum was something you built. Day by day. Touch by touch. One clear number and one time-blocked morning and one honest conversation at a time.

He got out of the car and walked toward his apartment, already thinking about tomorrow's list of names to call — the people who made him smile.

He had ten to reach.

* * *

PART II — FRAMING THE BUSINESS

Systems turn effort into momentum.

* * *

Part I poured the concrete. You clarified your numbers, anchored your days, and built a living CRM so your business no longer depended on memory and adrenaline alone. That work made the ground beneath you solid. But a foundation by itself doesn't move anyone. At some point, effort must start compounding. That is where framing begins.

Framing the business is about deciding how every major piece fits together so your actions no longer stand alone as isolated wins or losses. A great consultation here, a strong listing there, a flurry of follow-up next week — none of that creates real momentum if each moment lives in its own silo. Systems are what connect those moments so that one good conversation naturally leads to the next, a signed agreement flows into a predictable process, and a closing automatically becomes a long-term relationship instead of a dead end.

Most agents never make that shift. They stay stuck in a cycle where every transaction feels like a fresh start. Each buyer or seller requires them to reinvent how they explain the process, how they handle problems, and how they manage expectations. Their pipeline is full of names but not stages. Their calendar is full of tasks but not sequences. They are working hard, but nothing accumulates. The business feels like pushing a heavy cart with square wheels: tremendous effort, truly little glide.

In this part of the book, the goal is to change the shape of those wheels. You will define how people move through your world — from first contact, to consultation, to under contract, to closed, to nurtured for life. You will see what it means to have a pipeline that tells you exactly who is ready, who is warming up, and who needs a light touch instead of a hard push. You will create simple, repeatable buyer and seller experiences that remove improvisation from the moments that matter most.

Framing also reveals where leverage belongs. Once your processes are clear, you can finally see which parts truly require your voice and presence, and which parts can be carried by checklists, tools, or other people without sacrificing quality. Instead of handing off random tasks when you feel overwhelmed, you will delegate entire segments of a well-defined workflow. That is how systems start turning your effort into forward motion — not just temporary relief.

As you move through Part II, pay attention to how often the word *flow* shows up in your own thinking. Flow is what happens when your pipeline stages, processes, and communication rhythms line up so cleanly that volume no longer equals chaos. You are still working. Deals still require care. Problems still arise. But the work begins to feel connected. One stage leads to the next. One good week supports the one after it.

Systems will not remove the need for effort. They will decide what your effort becomes.

* * *

CHAPTER 8: The Pipeline Is a Measure of Readiness

A pipeline stage doesn't describe who someone is. It describes where they are.

* * *

By the time Mason revisited his CRM with Elias, something had changed.

The system no longer felt like a dumping ground for names.

It felt like a map.

He had names. He had notes. He had follow-up tasks assigned — most of them, anyway. But as he scrolled through the contacts, he noticed they all looked the same. Past clients sat next to new leads. People actively searching for homes were filed right next to someone who had mentioned, eight months ago, that they might want to sell someday. Everything felt equally important, which meant nothing felt clear.

Elias pulled his chair alongside Mason's desk and studied the screen for a moment.

"The problem isn't the CRM," Elias said. "The problem is that your pipeline doesn't have shape yet."

Mason looked at him. "What do you mean, shape?"

"Right now, every contact in here looks the same to you. So, your brain doesn't know whether to call this person urgently or just drop them a note. That ambiguity is exhausting. It's why follow-up feels like a chore — you're making the same decision over and over instead of just executing."

He leaned forward and pulled up a blank view of the pipeline stages.

"A pipeline stage doesn't describe who someone is," Elias said. "It describes where they are in the decision process."

That distinction settled over Mason like something finally clicking into place.

"So, the stage isn't a label."

"No. It's context. It tells you what kind of leadership this person needs from you right now. Not who they are as a person — where they are in the process."

Elias walked him through the categories.

Leads — new contacts who've entered the system, not yet engaged.

Attempting Contact — outreach has started, but no real two-way connection yet.

Hot — actively making decisions within the next three months. These people need your full attention and decisive guidance.

Warm — interested, but not deciding for another three to six months. They need consistent presence, not urgency.

Nurture — long-term relationship development for decisions six months or more away. Light touches, genuine care.

Sphere — personal and professional relationships who know you well. These are your most valuable contacts. Treat them accordingly.

Buyer — actively searching, signed agreement in place.

Seller — active listing, signed agreement in place.

Under Contract — transaction in progress.

Past Client — closed sale with an ongoing relationship. Never finished.

Professional Contact — vendors, lenders, attorneys, referral sources. Part of the ecosystem.

"Each stage answers one question," Elias said, tapping the screen. "How close is this person to taking action? And based on that answer, what's the right next move?"

Mason studied the list.

"So, the goal isn't to push everyone toward buying or selling as fast as possible?"

"No." Elias shook his head. "The goal is to meet people where they are and guide them appropriately. Pressure comes from confusion. When you don't know where someone is, you default to urgency — and that urgency reads as desperation, not leadership."

He paused to let that land.

"Confidence comes from clarity. When you know this person is in Nurture, you're not agonizing over whether to call them today. You're just staying in touch, sharing something useful, being present. When this person moves to Hot, you shift — more intentional, more proactive, more decisive. The stage tells you what role to play."

For the first time, Mason stopped feeling guilty about the contacts who weren't moving quickly. They weren't stuck. They simply weren't ready — yet. His job wasn't to force them forward. It was to make sure that when they were ready, he was the first person who came to mind. Because he was already staying in touch consistently, he'd recognize the moment their readiness shifted.

He updated his CRM that afternoon. Sorted. Tagged. Assigned stages. When he finished, the screen looked different. Calmer. It wasn't just a list anymore. It was organized by readiness, and readiness told him exactly what to do next.

* * *

The Conversation Math

With pipeline stages now mapping readiness, Elias walked Mason through the formula most agents never see — the one that turns the whole pipeline from a tracking tool into a production engine.

"Most agents think they need more leads," Elias said, pulling up a simple diagram. "What they actually need is more conversations."

He wrote out the formula.

20 conversations → 4 signed agreements → 2 closings →runway covered.

Mason stared at it. "That's it?"

"That's it. This formula doesn't demand perfection. It demands consistency. Twenty real, two-way conversations per week — not voicemails, not one-sided texts, not scrolling through someone's Instagram. Actual dialogue."

"And from twenty conversations, four people sign?"

"On average, when your process is solid. Some weeks more, some weeks fewer. But when you run this formula long enough, and you hold the inputs steady, the outputs start to smooth out. The spikes and valleys flatten. Your business stops depending on any single transaction to survive."

He circled the word *conversations.*

"Everything downstream — signings, contracts, closings — is a lagging indicator. By the time you close a deal, the work that created it was done weeks or months ago. Conversations are the leading indicator. They're the input you actually control."

Mason leaned back. "So, if my closings are slow, I don't look at my closings."

"Exactly. You look at your conversations from six weeks ago. That's what's showing up — or not showing up — today."

* * *

Three Channels

The twenty conversations didn't come from one place. Elias outlined three channels that together deliver nearly everything:

Sphere — past clients, family, friends, colleagues who know you. This channel generates roughly eighty percent of sustainable production for most agents. Not because these people always buy and sell. Because they refer, they trust, and they return. Sphere contacts don't need a sales pitch. They need consistent presence.

Pipeline Nurture — warm and hot contacts already in the system who are working toward a decision. These people are close. They need thoughtful follow-up, clear answers, and the sense that you're ready when they are.

New Leads — qualified contacts entering the system. New, but not random. Every new lead gets the same process: assessed, staged, assigned a next task, and worked consistently.

"These three channels work together," Elias said. "Your sphere keeps the business warm. Your pipeline nurture keeps it moving. New leads keep it growing."

* * *

Daily Execution

The morning block was non-negotiable.

Twenty conversations, front-loaded into the day before anything else had a chance to crowd them out. Ten sphere touches — people Mason already knew, checking in, adding value, staying present. Ten pipeline conversations — warm leads, hot buyers, sellers in prep, anyone with momentum building.

"The script doesn't need to be clever," Elias said. "Just human. *Hey, I was thinking about you. How's everything going?* That's enough. You're not calling to close. You're calling to connect."

Mason tracked it every day. Conversations logged. Pipeline stages updated. Notes written. Next tasks assigned before he moved on to anything else.

The formula wasn't complicated.

It just required showing up every morning and doing the work — twenty conversations at a time.

* * *

FOUNDATION MARKER

Leadership Window: Pipelines Do Not Create Pressure — They Remove It

When readiness is clear, your role becomes obvious. You stop guessing what each person needs and start leading them with precision. A clean pipeline isn't a management tool. It's an emotional regulation system for the agent.

You should now understand:

- How pipeline stages reflect readiness, not value or urgency
- Why categorizing contacts by stage improves follow-up quality and reduces decision fatigue
- The 20→4→2 conversation formula and why conversations are the only input that matters
- How sphere, pipeline nurture, and new leads work together as three distinct channels
- Why clarity in the pipeline creates confident leadership, not mechanical follow-up

* * *

CHAPTER 9: The Buyer Consultation

A consultation isn't a pitch. It's the beginning of a working relationship.

* * *

Ethan and Claire walked into the office on a Tuesday morning carrying the particular energy of people who had done too much research and not enough of it in the right direction.

They'd been online for weeks. They had a list of neighborhoods. They had screenshots of listings, some of which had already sold. They had a vague idea of their budget and an extremely specific idea of what their kitchen backsplash should look like.

Mason greeted them warmly, showed them to a pair of chairs, and then — instead of opening his laptop — asked them a question.

"Before we look at anything, can you tell me what brought you here today?"

Ethan and Claire exchanged a glance. They had expected the laptop. They had expected the tour of listings.

Claire spoke first. "We've been renting for four years. We want to stop throwing money away."

Mason nodded, unhurried. "What does owning feel like to you? What would change?"

That question opened something. They talked for a few minutes — about space, about stability, about a yard for their dog, about the feeling of having something that was actually theirs. Mason listened. Not waiting to respond. Actually listening.

Then he told them something they didn't expect.

"There is a process. My job is to walk you through it so that nothing feels confusing or reactive. But before I explain it, I want to make sure I understand how you move through decisions. Not just what you want to buy — how you want to feel when you buy it."

He asked more questions.

How do you start your mornings? Do you work from home, or commute? Do you cook, or do you order out most nights? What does a perfect Saturday at home look like? What would make a house feel like a relief, rather than one more thing to manage?

The conversation had a different texture than anything they'd expected. Warmer. More specific to them.

Only after he understood them did Mason walk them through the process.

He explained it simply, without rushing.

Understanding goals. Lifestyle, timeline, what's fixed and what's flexible.

Preparing financially. Comfort range versus maximum approval. How financial choices affect strategy in negotiation.

Searching intentionally. Why seeing fewer homes — chosen well — leads to better decisions and less fatigue.

Making offers strategically. How price, terms, and timing work together. How to stay calm when decisions need to be made quickly.

Navigating inspections and negotiations. What's normal? What's negotiable? How surprises get handled.

Closing with confidence. What happens in the final weeks, what to expect on closing day, and what support continues afterward.

"I've been through this process enough times to know where the questions usually come up," Mason said. "My job is to stay a step ahead of them, so you don't have to."

Ethan and Claire visibly relaxed.

Not because Mason promised them everything would be easy.

Because they felt oriented. Understood. Like they were in the hands of someone who'd been here before and wasn't in a hurry.

When they signed the buyer agency agreement and left, Mason stayed at the table for a moment.

Charlotte appeared in the doorway.

"How did it go?"

"Good," Mason said. "Better than good. They opened up quickly."

"Once they realized you weren't rushing them," Charlotte said, "they trusted the process." She paused. "Confidence isn't pretending. It's practicing until clarity becomes natural. You're there."

* * *

FOUNDATION MARKER

Leadership Window: Process Plus Curiosity Builds Trust

Guidance creates calm. Curiosity creates connection. Together, they create confidence. A buyer consultation is not where you display your knowledge — it's where you earn the right to guide someone through one of the most significant financial decisions of their life.

You should now understand:

- What a buyer consultation includes and why it happens before showing homes
- How asking lifestyle questions — not just logistics questions — builds deeper rapport
- How walking through the full buying process sets expectations and removes anxiety
- Why leading with process and curiosity earns trust faster than leading with expertise
- Why clients don't need perfection from their agent — they need leadership

* * *

CHAPTER 10: Listing Confidence Starts Before the Appointment

Preparation is not a step before the work. It is the work.

* * *

The call came from a neighbor of a past client.

Mr. Callahan had a bungalow three blocks from the water — cedar shake siding, a screened porch that caught the afternoon light, and hydrangeas that hadn't been pruned in two seasons. He'd lived there for eleven years. He wanted to sell by late spring, which gave Mason six weeks to earn the listing, prepare the property, and build a strategy he genuinely believed in.

Mason mentioned it to Charlotte that afternoon.

"Before you sit down with him," she said, "what do you know?"

Mason started to answer — neighborhood, price range, recent comps.

Charlotte shook her head gently. "That's not enough. Confidence doesn't come from knowing the neighborhood. It comes from knowing this property, this seller, and this market moment better than he does. Preparation is layered."

She walked him through the research process.

Public records and tax history. Permit information. Prior listing data for the property and neighboring homes. Neighborhood price trends over the last six, twelve, and eighteen months. Active listings that would compete directly. Days on market patterns. Condition differences between comparables.

"And when you go to the property," she added, "slow down. Really look at it. Not just what needs work — the light, the layout, how it feels to stand inside it. You're going to describe this home to buyers. You need to know it the way a buyer will experience it."

Mason took notes on a legal pad, the way he always did when Charlotte was teaching.

"There's also a two-step approach that removes the pressure from the initial appointment," she continued. "The first visit is a consultation — you listen, you learn, you build trust. You don't walk in with a pricing sheet. You walk in with questions. What improvements have you made? What do you love most about this place? What concerns you? Then you go back, do your analysis, and come back with data and a clear plan. You don't pitch before you understand."

"That seems like it would take more time," Mason said.

"It takes more intention. That's different. And it closes better — because by the time you present your strategy, you're not a salesperson. You're someone they already trust."

* * *

The Walkthrough

Mason drove to the Callahan property two days before the listing consultation.

Elias met him there.

They walked every room slowly. Elias had his tablet out, typing notes before Mason even knew what he was looking at. The list built quickly: paint touch-ups in the hallway and second bedroom. A sticky exterior door that needed the latch adjusted. Overgrown shrubs along the south fence. Mismatched light bulbs throughout. Clutter staged in the hallway that would read as cramped in photographs.

Mason looked at the list. "We don't have a lot of lead time."

"I never worry about time," Elias said. "I worry about process." He kept typing. "I'll schedule the handyman for Wednesday. Light staging can happen Thursday. Photography Friday morning, MLS input that afternoon. Everything has a runway."

"You can coordinate all of that?"

"That's why I'm here. You focus on communication and strategy. I manage logistics. You're the strategist. I'm the structure."

Mason exhaled something he hadn't known he was holding.

He'd been mentally bracing for the burden of coordinating all of it — the vendors, the timeline, the photography, the MLS prep. He'd assumed that's what listing agent did: carry all of it, all the time, alone.

He didn't have to carry the listing. He just had to lead it.

* * *

The Pricing Conversation

Two days later, Mason sat with Mr. Callahan at his kitchen table with the comp analysis spread across the surface between them.

The market had softened slightly. Buyers were more measured. Days on market had stretched in the neighborhood from an average of twelve to closer to twenty-eight. Two active competitors priced ten thousand above the logical range had already sat for six weeks without an offer.

Mason had thought carefully about how to open the pricing conversation. He chose to lead with honesty.

"Pricing is a strategy we build together," he said. "Not a number I hand you."

Mr. Callahan studied him. He'd worked with another agent on a rental property several years back — someone who had shown up with a number already written on a folder, as if the decision had been made before the conversation started.

"Tell me what you're seeing," Mr. Callahan said.

Mason walked him through the comps. He showed the recent solds — dates, adjusted sale prices, and condition notes. He showed the active competitors: the two overpriced properties still sitting, the one that had just reduced after thirty days. He explained condition differences — not critically, but factually. Here's what they had. Here's what you have. Here's how buyers make comparisons.

Then he talked about strategy.

"The market rewards accuracy. Too high and we lose the momentum of the first two weeks — and that's when the most serious buyers are watching. Too low and you leave money behind. What we're looking for is the number that attracts the right buyers quickly, creates urgency through early interest and positions us to negotiate from strength."

Mr. Callahan sat back in his chair and looked at the page for a long moment.

"That makes sense," he said. "I trust your judgment."

For the first time in his career, Mason didn't feel nervous during the pricing conversation.

He felt prepared.

There was a difference. Nervousness came from winging it. Confidence came from knowing.

* * *

The Launch

Elias texted Thursday evening: *Photography done. Clean. Really clean.*

Friday afternoon, Mason reviewed the full marketing file Elias had prepared. Professional photographs — the screened porch looked luminous, the kitchen was warm, the hydrangeas had been trimmed just enough to look intentional rather than neglected. The MLS description was precise and genuine. The marketing graphics matched the brokerage's brand standards. Everything looked consistent. Polished. Like a property that had been taken seriously.

Mason called Mr. Callahan to tell him the listing was live.

"It looks wonderful," Mr. Callahan said, after pulling it up on his phone. "You made it look like a real home."

"It is a real home," Mason said. "We just made sure the photos agreed."

He sat at his desk after the call and thought about what Charlotte had said.

Confidence doesn't come from delivery. It comes from preparation.

Not one layer of preparation. Layers. Research. Observation. A selling strategy grounded in data. A logistics system that didn't depend on him doing everything. A pricing conversation that had been a partnership, not a pitch.

All of it before the appointment.

All of it before the sign went in the yard.

* * *

FOUNDATION MARKER

Leadership Window: Preparation Creates Authority

Knowledge allows you to lead without selling. When you know more about a property and its market than the seller does, you don't need to be persuasive. You need to be clear. Clarity earns trust faster than confidence ever will.

You should now understand:

- How listing confidence is built through layered research before the appointment
- Why the two-step listing approach (consultation, then presentation) creates deeper trust
- How a property walkthrough with operations support reduces stress and raises quality
- How to frame a pricing conversation as a collaborative strategy, not a directive
- Why a well-prepared listing launch reflects on your professionalism long after the sale

* * *

CHAPTER 11: Compensation Conversations

Value explained calmly is rarely challenged.

* * *

Charlotte gathered the team on a Wednesday morning. Not a long meeting — she rarely held long meetings. Thirty minutes, four people, the conference table cleared.

"Compensation has changed," she said, sitting forward. "And I want to make sure every conversation you're having about fees is grounded in confidence, not apology."

She looked around the table. Mason. Two other agents. Elias in the doorway, arms folded, listening.

"Commission is negotiable in every direction now. Amount, structure, payer — it can all vary. That's not bad news. It's actually a clarifying moment. Because when there's no standard, the only thing that differentiates agents is the value they can articulate clearly."

She stood and wrote four things on the whiteboard:

Why you're worth what you charge? How you protect them. What outcomes you create. What risks you remove.

"That's what clients want to know," she said. "If you can't answer those four questions in plain language, you're going to struggle when someone pushes back on your fee. Not because the fee is wrong. Because you haven't earned the right to defend it yet."

The room was quiet. Not uncomfortable — attentive.

"Here's the shift I want you to make," Charlotte continued. "Stop leading with percentages. Start leading with process. Your fee isn't for paperwork. It's for leadership. It's for the preparation you did before the appointment, the strategy you built around the pricing conversation, the calm you bring when the inspection report comes in, and the buyer wants to walk. That's what you're being paid for."

She capped the marker.

"Your job is not to justify a fee. Your job is to articulate the service."

Mason wrote every word down.

* * *

What Clients Actually Fear

After the training, Mason walked back to his desk and sat with Charlotte's words for a while.

He thought about the moments he'd fumbled before — the quick disclosures, the half-apologies, the way he used to rush through the compensation explanation as if getting past it faster would make it hurt less. He'd been treating the conversation like a confrontation.

Charlotte had said: it's not a confrontation. It's information.

Clients weren't pushing back on the fee because they were hostile. They were pushing back because they didn't understand what they were buying. They had no context for what an agent actually did — not in their transaction, not in the specific work that would happen on their behalf between contract and close. They'd heard stories. They'd seen headlines. They were trying to make sense of a system that had publicly shifted.

The answer wasn't defensiveness. The answer was clarity.

He practiced it with Charlotte the following afternoon — a role-play conversation, a skeptical buyer, real objections.

"What do you charge?"

"My fee is structured this way." Clear. Direct.

"That seems like a lot."

"I understand. Let me show you what that covers." And then he walked through it — not in abstract terms, but specifically. The preparation before the consultation. The strategy built around their search. The fiduciary responsibility in every offer. The negotiation work when numbers don't align on the first try. The coordination during inspections, appraisals, the final walk-through. The answers to questions they didn't even know how to ask yet.

Charlotte listened. When he finished, she nodded.

"Better. Much better. But watch one thing — don't over-explain. When you over-explain, you sound like you're defending. When you're calm and concise, you sound like a professional who's done this many times."

* * *

The First Real Test

The chance to apply it came sooner than he expected.

Mason was wrapping up a buyer consultation — Ethan and Claire, a young couple who'd done too much research and not enough of it in the right direction. The meeting had gone well. He'd walked them through the process, set expectations, answered their questions with patience instead of urgency. They were nearly done — agreements reviewed, next steps clear — when Claire paused.

"So, what do buyer agents charge now? I heard it changed."

A month ago, that question would have tightened Mason's chest. He would have stumbled through an explanation, apologized for the complexity, tried to make the fee sound smaller.

This time, he took a single breath and answered.

"Every fee is negotiable now. There's no standard anymore." He kept his voice even. Matter of fact. "My job is to help you understand your options and structure something that fits your goals and your budget. Some buyers pay their agent directly. Many others request that the seller contribute to the buyer's agent compensation as part of the negotiation. We'll look at what makes the most sense for your situation."

Ethan and Claire nodded slowly.

"And yes," Mason added, "that conversation happens at the right stage of the process — not before we know what we're working with. I'll walk you through it when we get there."

They both relaxed.

Not because the answer removed all complexity. Because it removed the mystery. He'd given them a clear answer without making it sound like a problem.

Charlotte's voice echoed in his head: *Your job is not to justify a fee. Your job is to articulate the service.* He'd done exactly that. No apology. No defensiveness. Just clarity.

* * *

The Referral Call

Three weeks later, a new buyer reached out from a referral — someone Mason had never met, connected through a past client. She asked the question many buyers asked now.

"So how do agent fees work these days?"

Mason didn't tense up. He didn't rush.

"Great question. Because there's no standard anymore, we walk through a few options together. Some buyers pay their agent directly. Some request seller contributions during negotiation — and that's still very common. Some structure it creatively depending on their goals and budget. My job is to help you understand your choices and make sure we get you the best possible outcome."

The woman exhaled.

"That actually makes a lot of sense."

She scheduled a consultation for the following week. When she arrived, she was already at ease — there was no defensiveness in the room, no skepticism hanging over the first handshake. She'd been told up front that there were options, that the conversation was about her goals, that Mason's job was to guide rather than convince.

After she left with a signed agreement, Mason sat at his desk and recognized something he hadn't been able to name before.

Value wasn't about convincing. It was about guiding.

He wasn't defending anything. He was explaining a process — calmly, specifically, without apology. And when clients understood the process, the fee became part of the structure rather than an obstacle in front of it.

Charlotte had been right.

Value explained calmly is rarely challenged. Because it was never really the value being challenged. It was the confusion. And clarity had a way of dissolving that before it ever became a real problem.

* * *

FOUNDATION MARKER

Leadership Window: Value Explained Calmly Is Rarely Challenged

Confidence comes from clarity, not pressure. The agents who struggle with compensation conversations aren't struggling because their fee is wrong — they're struggling because they haven't practiced explaining the work behind it. Lead with process. Stay calm. Let the service speak for itself.

You should now understand:

- Why compensation conversations are about process and outcomes, not defense of a number
- How to articulate the four things clients actually want to know about your value
- How to shift from leading with percentages to leading with a description of service
- How calm, concise explanations reduce resistance faster than detailed justifications
- The arc from uncertainty to mastery: you learn the framework, then practice it until it becomes instinct

* * *

CHAPTER 12: Leverage Is What Allows You to Stay Human

The goal isn't to do more. The goal is to do what only you can do.

* * *

It arrived quickly — the way it always does when you've finally stopped doing things halfway.

Two buyers went under contract in the same week. A seller with a waterfront property wanted to prep for a spring launch. A past client called on Thursday to say she was finally ready to list, and could Mason meet with her the following Tuesday.

He stood at his desk looking at the calendar. Four active situations. Each one real. Each one needing him — or needing something.

The week before, this would have been exciting. This week, it was still exciting. But it was also the clearest look he'd had yet at the edge of his own bandwidth. He wasn't spiraling. But he could feel the way the pieces were starting to press against each other. A call here crowding out a follow-up there. A document review bleeding into his morning conversation block. The back-of-the-mind noise that came from tracking too many moving parts in one's head at once.

Instead of pushing through, he walked to Charlotte's office.

"I think I'm reaching capacity," he said.

She didn't look alarmed. She looked pleased.

"Good. That means you're ready for the next step."

* * *

Seeing Maya's Full Role

Mason had worked with Maya since his first weeks. She'd taught him to use his CRM properly, helped him build his contact system, and owned the post-closing relationship work that kept past clients connected to the team. He knew her as the person who made sure no one got lost.

What he hadn't fully understood — until Charlotte sat them down the next morning — was the other half of Maya's role.

"You've seen how Maya manages the relationship side," Charlotte said. "Now you need to see how she manages the transaction side. Because that's what's going to free you up."

Maya sat across from Mason with a tablet in her hand and the kind of calm that comes from someone who has genuinely figured out her job. Not the practiced calm of someone performing confidence — the real kind.

"Here's the part you haven't been using yet," Maya said.

She walked through her contract-to-close process.

Inspection coordination — scheduling, attending when needed, following up with the inspector and both parties. Appraisal tracking — monitoring the order, flagging if timelines slipped, keeping Mason and the client informed. Document management — every form, every amendment, every addendum tracked and filed. Compliance checks at each milestone. Communication timelines so no client went more than a few days without an update. Attorney and lender coordination. Weekly client progress reports so buyers and sellers always knew where they stood.

Mason stared at the list.

"That's... a lot."

Maya smiled. She'd clearly heard this before.

"That's my job. I handle the details so you can stay focused on serving, negotiating, and generating business."

He exhaled slowly. "I didn't realize how much time I was losing trying to manage all of that myself."

"You weren't losing time," she said, with the same gentleness she applied to everything. "You were learning. Now you're ready for the next level."

* * *

The Relief of Structure

A week later, in the middle of a Tuesday afternoon, Mason found himself juggling updates between his two buyers under contract. Inspection date for one, appraisal follow-up for the other. Attorney updates pending. He was staring at his phone, trying to reconstruct the sequence of conversations from memory, when Maya appeared beside him.

"Need help?" she asked.

"Yes." He didn't hesitate. "I think I'm starting to drop things."

She sat down and pulled up the contract-to-close report for both transactions.

"Here's where we are for the Hendersons — inspection complete, report delivered, repairs requested. I've already sent their weekly update. Lender confirmed appraisal is scheduled for Thursday."

She swiped to the second file.

"For the Garcias — appraisal came in on value, attorney is drafting closing disclosures. I've confirmed the walk-through for next Monday. I emailed them this morning."

Mason blinked.

"You did all that already?"

"That's my job."

He looked at her. Then at the screen. Then back at her.

Something shifted. Not dramatically — not in the way large realizations tend to arrive loudly. Quietly. Like a door he hadn't known was locked quietly swinging open.

He wasn't just becoming a better agent.

He was becoming a supported one.

* * *

What Elias Added

That afternoon, Elias stopped by his desk.

"You seem lighter," Elias said.

"I finally sat down with Maya on the contract side this week. Actually, let her run it."

Elias gave a small nod. "Good. And don't forget — if you ever want help prepping listings faster, that's on my side. Any time."

Mason raised an eyebrow. "You help with listing prep?"

"Coordinating vendors, managing photography timelines, MLS input, marketing file, staging scheduling. That's one of my favorite parts." He looked completely unbothered by the scope of it. "You focus on strategy. I manage logistics."

Mason sat with that for a moment.

"And I've been trying to do all of that alone?"

"Not anymore," Elias said.

* * *

The Real Meaning of Leverage

That evening, Mason drove home along the coast highway with the windows down. The salt air came in off the water, and he thought about the phrase Charlotte had used in one of their early meetings: *leverage lets you serve more people without losing yourself.*

He understood it theoretically then. He understood it differently now.

Leverage wasn't about stepping back from the business. It was about standing where he was strongest. The relationship — that was his. The strategy — his. The negotiation, the consultation, the moment when a client needed someone steady to remind them that the process was working even when it felt uncertain — his.

Everything else? Everything that could be handled by someone with a system designed for exactly that purpose — that was the waste. Not because those things didn't matter. They mattered enormously. The details that Maya tracked kept clients from feeling forgotten. The logistics that Elias managed kept listings from looking unprepared. These things shaped the client experience just as much as the conversations Mason had in person.

They just didn't require Mason to carry them personally.

That was the distinction. Leverage wasn't abandonment. It wasn't passing off what mattered to someone who cared less. It was recognizing what each person on the team was built to do — and trusting them to do it, so Mason could do his part at full capacity instead of fractional capacity.

He pulled into his driveway and sat for a moment before going inside.

Busy didn't have to mean frantic. If it did, the system wasn't finished.

His was getting closer to finished every week.

* * *

FOUNDATION MARKER

Leadership Window: Leverage Protects What Matters Most

When the backend is supported, the front end can stay human. Delegation is not a sign that you can't handle your business — it is proof that you understand what your business actually needs from you. The agent's job is relationships, strategy, and trust. Everything else is infrastructure.

You should now understand:

- What leverage means in a real estate context — not doing more, but doing the right things
- How contract-to-close coordination (CTC) functions and what it covers
- How operations support from a director of operations changes the listing experience
- Why leverage increases your presence with clients, not your distance from them
- That "reaching capacity" is not a warning sign — it's a signal that you're ready for the next level of structure

* * *

CHAPTER 13: Metrics That Tell You What to Fix

Numbers don't judge. They point.

* * *

Mason used to check his numbers the way some people check the weather in a storm — already bracing for what he'd find.

Good week? He exhaled. Caught up on everything he'd been putting off. Ate well, slept fine.

Slow week? The anxiety settled in around Tuesday and stayed through the weekend. He second-guessed conversations. Replayed listing appointments. Wondered whether the strategy was working or whether he'd been fooling himself about his own progress.

The numbers weren't a tool. They were a verdict.

Elias dismantled that in a single meeting.

He pulled up Mason's weekly dashboard on a Monday morning — not at the end of a tough week, not as damage control, but as the ordinary rhythm of running the business.

"Metrics aren't a scoreboard," he said. "They're a diagnostic tool. They don't tell you if you're good or bad. They tell you where to focus next."

He held Mason's gaze for a moment.

"You don't fix results. You fix inputs. And inputs are what the metrics actually measure."

* * *

The Seven Metrics

Elias walked through each one.

Metric 1: Conversations per Week.

The foundation. Not voicemails. Not unanswered texts. Two-way exchanges — phone calls where both parties talk, meaningful texts with replies, in-person meetings, DMs with real back-and-forth.

"If closings drop, most agents go straight to 'I need more leads,'" Elias said. "But usually the answer is simpler: conversations dropped six weeks ago, and this week's closings are the echo. Fix the conversations. Everything else follows."

Metric 2: Follow-Up Completion Rate.

Follow-ups completed ÷ follow-ups scheduled × 100.

Forty follow-ups scheduled. Thirty-two completed. Eighty percent.

"Ninety percent or above is strong. Between seventy and eighty-nine, you're inconsistent. Below seventy, you have relationship leakage — people who expected to hear from you and didn't. Most deals aren't lost because of skill. They're lost because of silence." If follow-up completion is low, don't add more leads. Fix execution first.

Metric 3: Pipeline Volume.

The count of contacts at each stage. Not a total number — a breakdown.

Leads: 25. Attempting Contact: 18. Hot: 2. Warm: 14. Under Contract: 3.

"A healthy business has depth, not just activity," Elias said. "If everything is clustered at one stage, flow breaks. Thin front end means you need more outreach. No mid-pipeline means your nurture is slipping. A bottleneck just before Under Contract usually means there's a conversion skill to tighten."

Metric 4: Stage Conversion Rate.

(Contacts that advanced ÷ contacts in previous stage) × 100.

Twenty leads contacted. Six became signed clients. Thirty percent conversion.

"Low conversion isn't always a lead problem. Usually it's a clarity problem — something in the consultation, the follow-up, or the process explanation isn't landing the way it should. The metric tells you where to look. It doesn't tell you what to feel about it."

Metric 5: Contracts Written vs. Conversations.

(Contracts written ÷ total conversations) × 100.

"This one shows traction. One hundred twenty conversations, four contracts — 3.3%. As your systems improve, this number rises naturally. Watch it over time, not in any single week."

Metric 6: Closed Transactions per Month.

The lagging indicator. The one everyone watches too closely.

"Closings confirm the system worked — past tense. They reflect work done weeks or months earlier. Never try to fix closings directly. Fix what leads to them."

Metric 7: Time-to-Decision (Cycle Time).

Total days from first contact to contract ÷ number of clients.

"Long cycle times are informative. They usually mean unclear expectations set early, or a hesitation that wasn't addressed in the consultation. When this number stretches, go back to how you explain the process at the beginning. That's almost always where the delay is seeded."

* * *

The Weekly Review

Elias gave Mason a rule for using these numbers.

"Never look at them without deciding what they mean."

Three questions at the end of every week:

What moved forward?

What stalled?

What input needs adjusting next week?

No emotion. No shame. Just clarity.

Mason started his first weekly review that Friday. He sat with the dashboard for twenty minutes — not anxiously, but methodically. Conversations were strong. Follow-up completion was at seventy-eight percent: room to tighten. Pipeline volume looked healthy at the top, thinner in the mid-stages than he wanted. He set a task for the following Monday: fifteen nurture calls, warm leads who hadn't heard from him recently.

He didn't feel relief when the review ended. He didn't feel dread when it started. He felt something simpler and more useful: direction.

* * *

The P&L Review

Two weeks later, Charlotte pulled him into her office.

"It's time for your first P&L review," she said.

She opened his spreadsheet. GCI earned to date. Brokerage splits. Marketing spend. Business expenses: MLS, subscriptions, vehicle costs, training, client gifts. Taxes reserved. Net profit.

Mason looked at the numbers. He expected to feel exposed — the way he'd always felt when finances came up, that low-grade anxiety that there would be something wrong, something he'd missed.

Instead, he felt something unexpected.

"This is a lot better than I thought."

Charlotte smiled. "Because you're doing the right things. And you're not overspending."

She pointed to the net profit column. "This is the number that matters. Not your GCI. Not your gross commissions. What actually remains after the business does its work."

"It makes it feel real," Mason said. "Like I'm actually running a business."

"You are," Charlotte said. "You've been running one for months. You're just now seeing the proof."

They built the weekly review rhythm together in that meeting. Not an end-of-month reckoning. Not an annual surprise. A recurring rhythm — every week, a pulse check on the leading indicators; every quarter, a clear-eyed look at the full P&L.

Metrics replaced the anxiety only when they became routine.

When numbers stopped being events and started being information, Mason stopped bracing for them.

He started trusting them instead.

* * *

FOUNDATION MARKER

Leadership Window: Metrics Create Calm When You Trust Them

Clarity removes fear faster than motivation ever will. The agents who dread their numbers are usually the agents who look at them least often. The more regularly you review, the less dramatic it feels. And the less dramatic it feels, the faster you can make adjustments before small problems become real ones.

You should now understand:

- The seven key metrics that actually diagnose the health of a real estate business
- How to calculate each metric and what benchmark to aim for • Why metrics are leading and lagging indicators — and why that distinction matters
- How to conduct a weekly review without emotion, using three simple questions
- How a P&L review shifts your relationship with your business from anxious to ownership

* * *

FOUNDATION IN PRACTICE — PART II

When Flow Replaced Force

* * *

Before he understood his pipeline, Mason treated everyone the same.

Every lead received urgency. Every silence felt personal. Every slow week felt like an indictment.

He was working hard. He was staying consistent, mostly. But the effort moved in one direction only — outward, with no real structure to catch what came back.

Then the framing started.

Contacts sorted by readiness: Hot, Warm, Nurture, Sphere. Each stage telling him exactly what the relationship needed — not pressure, not silence, but the right kind of presence at the right moment. His follow-up became appropriate instead of frantic. When someone moved slowly, Mason no longer took it personally. He knew which stage they were in, and he knew what to do while they were there.

Buyer consultations became calmer. Not because Mason had memorized a better script, but because he had a genuine process to walk through — one he believed in, one he could explain with the steady voice of someone who had thought it through carefully before stepping into the room.

Listings improved because preparation replaced improvisation. Elias's walkthrough checklist. Layered research. The pricing conversation as partnership. A launch that looked professional because every step had a place in a system that had been working before Mason arrived.

The compensation conversations that had once made him tense became matter-of-fact. Not overnight. But through repetition — Charlotte's training, practice with real clients, the gradual accumulation of evidence that calm clarity worked better than anxious defense.

And when bandwidth tightened, Mason didn't scramble alone. He walked to Charlotte. He met with Maya. He let Elias take the logistics of the listing. He stopped treating help as a sign of weakness and started treating it as architecture — load-bearing support that made the whole structure stronger.

The metrics told him what to fix. Not in a way that stung, but in a way that pointed. Conversations low? Start there. Follow-up completion slipping? That's the lever. P&L looking better than expected? Keep the same inputs because they're working.

Flow replaced force.

Not because Mason worked less hard. Because the structure absorbed the effort and turned it into something sustainable.

He still had hard days. He still had slow weeks and complicated negotiations and sellers who needed more patience than the timeline allowed. But the work felt different now. Connected. One stage leading to the next. One good week building the foundation for the one that followed.

Mason sat at his desk one evening after everyone else had gone and looked at the pipeline spread across his screen. Hot, Warm, Nurture, Sphere. Under Contract in two places. Past Clients growing in number, every one of them with a task, a note, a next action. The CRM wasn't a list. It was a living record of relationships that were being tended.

He thought about where he'd been when this all started — the feeling that the business was holding its breath, that every win required a sprint, that nothing was anchored.

He thought about Charlotte's phrase from those first weeks: *you need a foundation.*

He understood now what she meant. Not just the literal foundation of burn rates and CRM setup. The whole structure: pipeline clarity, buyer process, listing preparation, compensation confidence, leverage, metrics. All of it together, load bearing and connected, turning his effort into something that compounded.

The question was no longer whether the foundation could hold.

The question was how much weight it could carry

PART III — WEIGHT-BEARING GROWTH

Can this structure carry more weight?

* * *

Part I established that a business without a foundation will always feel fragile, no matter how hard you work. Part II showed how framing your systems and processes can turn that work into genuine momentum instead of isolated wins. Together, they created stability and flow. But eventually, every real estate business runs into the same question: can this carry more weight?

Markets shift constantly — rates climb and fall, inventory tightens or floods, headlines flip from boom to bust. These cycles have played out for decades. The real surprise isn't the change itself, but how often agents treat each new wave as if it's never happened before. When you stay proactive — maintaining consistent lead generation, tracking pipeline depth, and keeping clients informed on what's normal — most "crises" become predictable adjustments, not emergencies. The market stays unpredictable. Your business stays steady.

Weight-bearing growth is the moment when most businesses are exposed. Not because the agent suddenly becomes less talented or less driven, but because the structure underneath was never designed for volume. The same habits that worked at three closings a month start to crack at six. What once felt like healthy urgency turns into constant strain. Follow-up slips. Boundaries blur. Client experience becomes inconsistent. Growth doesn't create the problems; it reveals the ones that were already there.

This part of the book exists to make sure that revelation works in your favor. Here, growth is treated not as a rush of opportunity to chase, but as pressure your systems should be able to hold. You will see what happens when daily conversations, pipeline depth, and CRM follow-up stay steady even as the market shifts. You will explore how to raise your price point without abandoning the clients who built your business, and how to widen your reach without thinning out your integrity. The goal is simple: more volume, same calm. More complexity, same clarity.

Weight-bearing growth also tests your relationship with leverage. When your foundation and framing are solid, adding support — people, tools, or both — stops being a reaction to overwhelm and becomes a strategic choice. You will learn how to let systems and partners carry the load they were designed to carry, so that your time and emotional bandwidth stay focused on the work only you can do: leadership, negotiation, and deepening trust with the people you serve. Growth, in this context, isn't about squeezing more hours out of your day. It's about expanding the capacity of the business without shrinking your life.

By the time you move through Part III, the question is no longer, "Can I handle this?" It becomes, "Is the structure ready for what I'm asking it to hold?" That shift is the essence of sustainability. A business that can bear weight doesn't just survive busy seasons or market swings — it stays steady enough that you can keep showing up the same way: present, prepared, and consistent. This part of the journey isn't about chasing more for its own sake. It's about proving that what you've built can grow without breaking the very things that made it worth building in the first place.

* * *

CHAPTER 14: Your First Busy Season

Your first busy season arrives the moment you're ready to handle it.

* * *

Everyone told Mason that December would be slow.

The market cools, they said. Buyers pause for the holidays. Sellers wait until the new year. Enjoy the quiet while you have it. He'd heard it from agents at open houses, from colleagues in the bullpen, even from a mentor outside the team who had been in the business long enough to have seen every version of this prediction come and go.

By the first week of December, Mason was no longer sure they had been talking about the same business he was building.

His phone lit up before eight most mornings. His CRM was cycling through follow-ups he'd planted in September and October — warm touches that were now flowering into real conversations. A lender partner was sending referrals. Two past clients had called with questions about neighbors who wanted to sell. A buyer from a fall consultation, someone who had gone quiet for six weeks, had texted: *We're ready. Can we look this weekend?*

He was juggling multiple active buyers, two listings in preparation, two clients already under contract, a stream of inbound referrals, and showings booked most afternoons. Holiday cards needed to go out. Market updates needed to reach his sphere. And somewhere in there, Christmas was happening.

It wasn't chaos.

But it was a lot. And the weight of it was different from any load he'd carried before — not because it was heavier, but because it was *sustained.* There was no single crisis demanding his attention. There were six good things happening simultaneously, and each of them deserved care he wasn't sure he could fully give.

This time — unlike the version of himself from months ago who would have absorbed the pressure silently until something broke — Mason recognized the signs early.

He walked straight into Charlotte's office.

"I think I need help," he said. Simple as that.

Charlotte looked up from her desk. She didn't look surprised. She looked satisfied.

"That sentence," she said, "is what separates average agents from scalable agents."

She set down her pen. "Most agents wait until they're drowning before they say that. By then, they're already underwater, and everything they hand off has damage attached to it. You came in before the water was at your chin. That matters."

She pushed her chair back and gestured for him to sit.

"Walk me through it."

They pulled out Mason's workload together and spread it across the table — active files, pipeline stages, upcoming needs, Maya's timeline board. Charlotte was quiet for a moment as she took it in. Then she looked up at him with the particular clarity of someone who had solved this exact problem many times before.

"Your foundation is holding," she said. "But you're at capacity. This is the moment every growing agent reaches." She tapped the table. "It's not a sign to panic. It's a sign to leverage."

Mason nodded. He knew what that word meant now, not just as a concept, but as a lived practice. Maya handled contract coordination. Elias owned listing support. The systems took care of the repetitive work. His energy was reserved for the conversations, decisions, and relationships that genuinely required him.

He also knew what Charlotte was going to say next.

"Now we find out whether you've built a business... or just borrowed some free time."

Five days after the listing launched, the team gathered for their weekly operations meeting. It was the Callahan listing, the one Elias had coordinated down to the final photo angle, and the one Mason had checked in on twice that week to make sure Mr. Callahan felt informed and confident at every step.

The meeting was wrapping up when Mason's phone buzzed.

He glanced down.

Appraisal low. Need to discuss.

His stomach tightened.

He read the message twice.

Then a third time.

Five days under contract. A strong offer. A seller who was relieved and already planning his next chapter. And now this.

The appraisal had come in below the contract price. Not by a catastrophic margin, but enough to matter. Enough to put the transaction at risk.

This was new territory. He had discussed appraisal challenges with Charlotte. He had covered them in training. He knew, in theory, that they happened every day.

But theory and reality were two different things.

This wasn't just another transaction.

This was Mr. Callahan's home. Mason's reputation. A buyer who had stretched to make the offer work.

For a moment, the room was quiet.

The old version of Mason would have hurried back to his desk, called the seller before he fully understood the situation, and spent the next two days trying to solve every piece of the problem himself while silently hoping it all worked out.

Instead, he looked around the conference table.

"We've got a low appraisal on the Callahan property."

No one panicked.

No one looked to Charlotte for permission.

They simply went to work.

"I'll pull the appraisal," Elias said. "Let's see what we're dealing with."

"I'll review the contract dates," Maya added. "If this pushes closing, I'll have an extension ready before anyone asks."

Charlotte nodded toward the conference room.

"Let's spread everything out."

Within minutes, the appraisal report covered the table.

Together, they worked through it, not with urgency, but with the calm focus of people solving a problem instead of reacting to one.

The comparable sales told the story.

Two of the properties the appraiser had used were geographically close but fundamentally different from Mr. Callahan's home. They offered different water access, smaller lots, older construction, and a different buyer profile altogether. Meanwhile, a recent sale just three streets away, nearly identical in location, condition, and features, had been omitted entirely.

Elias tapped the report.

"That's not a bad market," he said. "That's an incomplete analysis."

Charlotte nodded.

"Then we answer it with evidence. No emotion. No opinions. Just facts."

The rest of the afternoon became a coordinated effort.

Elias assembled the supporting comparable sales and organized every piece of market data needed for a formal Reconsideration of Value packet. Charlotte drafted the narrative, calm, factual, and written in the language lenders and appraisers respected.

Maya worked through the contract timeline.

"If the review takes longer than expected," she said, "I'll have a closing extension drafted and ready. Hopefully we won't need it, but if we do, we're prepared."

That left Mason with the one responsibility no one else could own.

The seller.

Driving home that evening, he realized something that would have been impossible a year earlier.

He wasn't trying to become an appraiser.

He wasn't trying to become a contract coordinator.

He wasn't trying to become an operations manager.

His team had carried those pieces.

Now he could carry his.

When he called Mr. Callahan that evening, he wasn't searching for answers.

He had them.

"Here's what we know," Mason said. He explained how the appraisal had been developed, the comparable sales that had been overlooked, the reconsideration process, and the possible outcomes. He also explained what the next steps would be if the value only partially increased.

Mr. Callahan listened quietly.

Finally he asked, "So... what's our plan?"

Mason smiled.

"We've already built it."

Three days later, the reconsideration came back.

The value increased. Not all the way to the contract price, but enough to narrow the gap. A short negotiation followed. Buyer and seller each gave a little. The deal stayed together and closed on schedule.

The seller was relieved.

The buyers were relieved.

Even the lender seemed relieved.

As Mason locked his office that evening, he realized what he was feeling wasn't relief.

It wasn't luck.

It wasn't simply surviving another transaction.

It was competence.

Not because he had solved the problem alone.

Because he no longer had to.

* * *

Charlotte stopped by his desk later that afternoon.

"This is the moment most agents break," she said quietly. "They get busy, something goes sideways, and everything collapses — because the load was only ever being held by one pair of hands."

She glanced toward the conference room where the reconsideration paperwork was still sitting.

"You didn't break. You knew where to go. You knew what to build."

Mason looked at her. "The systems worked."

"You worked," she said. "The systems carried the rest."

That distinction mattered more than he expected. He had shown up, made the calls, had the conversations, and led the process. The systems — Maya's timelines, Elias's research discipline, Charlotte's coaching frameworks, the process they'd built around reconsiderations — had carried the weight that would have buried him alone.

This was what the foundation was for.

Not to make the job easy.

To make it *holdable.*

* * *

FOUNDATION MARKER

Leadership Window

The first real pressure test reveals whether the foundation was built or merely assembled. When systems hold under weight, it is because someone built them carefully enough to carry it. Calm, in a crisis, is not a personality trait. It is a product of preparation.

You should now understand:

- Why the first busy season is a diagnostic, not a crisis — it reveals what your systems can and cannot hold
- How to approach an appraisal gap as a process problem rather than an emotional emergency
- That seeking help early is a sign of professional maturity, not weakness
- Why leverage — people, systems, and clear roles — protects the client experience during high-volume periods
- How calm under pressure is built in advance, not summoned in the moment

* * *

CHAPTER 15: Delegation Is Leadership

Delegation is not loss — it is leadership.

* * *

The December workload hadn't fully settled when Charlotte brought it up again.

Mason was back in her office two days later, this time with his pipeline open on his laptop. Active buyers, listings in motion, pending closings, follow-ups stacking for the week ahead. He had managed to hold everything together through the appraisal situation, and the relief of the resolution was real. But holding everything wasn't the same as doing everything well. Charlotte had been watching long enough to know the difference.

"Tell me about your buyers," she said.

He walked through them. Two were under contract and in Maya's capable hands. One was actively searching and needed showings every weekend. And then there was Caroline Briggs.

First-time buyer. Thirty-one years old, recently relocated to the area for work, buying alone for the first time. Eager and anxious in equal measure. She texted frequently — not with problems exactly, but with the small, recurring need for reassurance that every unfamiliar step produced. *Is this normal? Should I be worried about this? What does that mean?*

She wasn't difficult. She was simply present in the way that first-time buyers often are — fully alive to every new development and needing someone to help her understand each one.

The problem was Mason's mornings were already spoken for. His afternoons were stacked with showings for two other buyers. His evenings belonged to follow-up, listing updates, and the calls that always seemed to find him between six and eight.

He looked up from his laptop.

"Lily," Charlotte said, before he could finish the thought.

He'd been working alongside Lily Chen for three months. She was newer to the team than Mason — had joined in the fall with a year of residential experience at another brokerage, quieter by nature but meticulous with her follow-up, the kind of agent who logged every conversation and never missed a scheduled task in her CRM. She'd closed two deals in her first three months. She was ready for a third.

"She has the right personality for Caroline," Charlotte said. "Patient, warm, thorough. She has the availability you don't. And she needs the experience." Charlotte paused. "The most important person in this conversation is Caroline. What's best for her?"

Mason already knew the answer.

He also felt the resistance. It wasn't doubt in Lily. It was something closer to ownership — the feeling that handing a client to someone else meant something had gone wrong, that he had failed to plan well enough, that Caroline had come to him specifically and deserved *him* specifically.

Charlotte read it in his face.

"Delegation isn't abandonment," she said. "It's a decision about where your value is highest. Caroline needs full attention right now. You can't give her that. Lily can. And in six months, when you're managing even more volume, this is going to happen again. You need to practice it now, when the stakes are manageable."

* * *

He called Caroline that afternoon.

He didn't hedge. He didn't over-explain or apologize for something that wasn't an error. He spoke the way Charlotte had coached him to speak from the beginning — warmly, clearly, with confidence behind every word.

"Caroline, I want to make sure you have the best possible experience through this process," he said. "My teammate Lily has exactly the right personality and availability to be your day-to-day point of contact. I'll still be overseeing everything and available for any bigger conversations or decisions, but Lily will be with you every step of the way."

A beat of silence.

"That actually sounds wonderful," Caroline said. Her voice was lighter than he'd heard it in weeks.

He exhaled quietly.

"I'll introduce you both today."

* * *

He found Lily at her desk before the afternoon was over. She had her headphones in, working through something in her CRM, a cup of tea beside her laptop that had gone cold without her noticing. She pulled her headphones out when she saw him approach.

Mason explained what he was handing her — the full context of Caroline's situation, her timeline, her concerns, the particular kind of attention she needed at this stage.

Lily went very still as she listened.

When he finished, she looked at him for a long moment.

"You trust me with a buyer?" she said softly.

"I trust you with *this* buyer," Mason replied. "And you're ready."

Something shifted in her. It was visible — the kind of change that doesn't take very long but that you can see clearly when you're watching for it. Her shoulders straightened. Her chin came up. She turned back to her laptop with a new kind of focus.

"I won't let you down," she said.

He watched her pull up Caroline's file, study the notes he'd left, and begin composing the introduction text. And he felt something unexpected move through him.

Not just relief that a scheduling problem had been solved.

Pride.

Not pride in what he had done. Pride in what he had *given*. In the space he had created for someone else to grow into. The opportunity he had placed in Lily's hands — not because it was easy or because he had no other choice, but because he had recognized she was ready and believed that the best thing he could do for everyone involved was to trust that.

That feeling was new.

A good new.

* * *

With Caroline in Lily's hands and Maya managing contract timelines for the two active transactions, something happened to Mason's mind that he hadn't fully experienced since starting this business.

It cleared.

Not empty — he still had work, still had clients, still had Mr. Callahan's post-closing follow-up to coordinate and two buyer searches to advance and a pipeline that needed his attention. But the mental clutter that had accumulated over weeks of trying to hold every thread simultaneously, of being the single point of contact for every need across every file — that was gone.

He could feel the difference in how he approached his mornings. He wasn't opening his laptop and immediately bracing for what had arrived overnight. He was opening it and choosing where to focus.

He shifted from reacting to planning. From scrambling to scheduling. From doing everything to doing the right things.

And then — because timing in real estate is never subtle — a seller reached out wanting to list fast. Someone who had been watching Mason's recent market video and felt ready to make a move before the new year, before rates shifted again, before the moment passed.

Old Mason would have panicked. Would have tried to absorb it, added it to the pile, stayed up late trying to coordinate everything himself.

New Mason walked straight to Elias.

"I need your help prepping a new listing," he said.

Elias smiled. Not the smile of someone surprised. The smile of someone who had been waiting for this exact moment.

"Great," he said. "Let's get started."

Over the following week, Mason watched the listing system come alive. Punch list completed in two days. Staging coordinated with a local firm Elias had worked with for years — in and out in a morning. Vendors scheduled, photographers booked at the right light, MLS data built, marketing pieces queued and ready for the day of launch. The whole operation moved in sequence, each element leading cleanly to the next.

Mason's role was lighter and clearer than he'd ever experienced in a listing:

Communicate with the seller. Refine the pricing strategy. Call the warm leads in his pipeline who might be matches for this property. Film a preview video. Oversee the launch plan.

At one point, he stood in the doorway of Elias's workspace, watching him move through a checklist with quiet efficiency.

"This isn't magic," Elias said, without looking up.

"I know," Mason said. "It's process."

Elias glanced back at him. "You're learning."

A great team doesn't remove responsibility. It removes chaos. And in the space where the chaos had been, there was finally room to lead.

Mason thought about the version of himself who had resisted all of this — who had believed, somewhere underneath his professionalism, that doing it all himself was the proof that he was doing it right. That needing help was a crack in the foundation rather than a feature of how strong foundations were built.

He didn't believe that anymore.

Leading meant putting the right people in the right roles and trusting them fully. It meant resisting the urge to carry weight that wasn't yours to carry. It meant recognizing, finally, that what clients needed wasn't access to every hour of your day. They needed someone who showed up clear, focused, and unencumbered.

Delegation made that possible.

Leadership was what it looked like.

* * *

FOUNDATION MARKER

Leadership Window

Delegation multiplies capacity without dividing quality. The agent who learns to hand off well doesn't lose a client — they gain a colleague who rises to meet the trust placed in them. True leadership is not doing more. It is creating the conditions for others to do well.

You should now understand:

- When delegation is the right decision — not as a last resort, but as a strategic choice made before the situation becomes urgent
- How to communicate a handoff to a client in a way that builds confidence rather than concern
- Why receiving a delegated client is an act of trust that elevates the person receiving it
- How operational support frees strategic capacity — and why this is not a shortcut but a skill
- That shifting from "doing everything" to "doing the right things" is the beginning of real leadership

* * *

CHAPTER 16: The Turning Point

The moment you stop pretending is the moment you start leading.

* * *

Mason sat in his car for a long time after the appraisal closed.

The parking lot outside the office had emptied while he'd been inside finishing the last of the paperwork. The coastal air had shifted — that particular December change along the North Carolina shoreline when the warmth finally gives way and the evenings start carrying real cold. He could hear the wind off the water from where he sat.

He wasn't on the phone. He wasn't reviewing his pipeline or answering messages or planning the next thing. He wasn't doing any of the things he usually filled the quiet with.

He was just sitting with what had happened.

He ran through it the way you might watch footage of yourself — the appraisal email arriving, the stomach drop, the decision he'd made in that moment to walk to Charlotte and Elias instead of spiraling alone. The way they had spread the report across the table and worked through it methodically, without drama. The call Mr. Callahan. The reconsideration. The outcome.

He thought about who had been in the room. Elias, pulling the data with the calm efficiency of someone who had done this dozens of times. Charlotte, drafting the narrative with precision. Maya, preparing the extension addendum before it was even needed. Mason himself, leading the seller conversation.

No one had panicked. No one had improvised. No one had made it up as they went.

And then, quietly, a realization settled in.

Neither had he.

He hadn't been scared.

He hadn't been improvising. He hadn't been guessing. He hadn't been white-knuckling his way through it with the secret fear that he was one wrong sentence away from losing the deal and the client and whatever credibility he'd spent the last year building.

He had been *leading*.

With clarity. With systems. With support. With a calm he hadn't manufactured — one that had grown, without his fully noticing, out of months of doing the right things in the right order so that when something hard arrived, there was structure underneath him to stand on.

He whispered it to the empty car, to no one:

"This is who I'm becoming."

Not the version of himself who had walked into Charlotte's office eight months ago with a full calendar and a fragile foundation. Not the agent who had treated every closing like a lucky event and every slow week like a personal indictment. Not the version that had confused activity for intention and busyness for progress.

This version.

He didn't know how long he'd been sitting there when he finally turned the key.

* * *

He almost missed it entirely.

He had come back inside to gather his things — laptop bag, notepad, the coffee mug he always forgot and always retrieved the next morning — when he heard voices in the hallway near the back of the suite. Charlotte and Elias, talking quietly. The door to the operations room was half open, sound carrying easily in the empty office.

He wasn't trying to listen. He simply stopped walking.

"He's ready for higher volume," Elias said.

A brief pause.

Charlotte's reply came measured and clear. "If he keeps his systems, yes. He's consistent. He listens. He applies." Another pause. "That's rare."

Mason stood completely still.

They weren't saying this to encourage him. They weren't performing it in his direction, the way that well-meaning praise sometimes works — said to someone's face with the effect of making them feel better in the moment. This was a professional conversation, the kind Charlotte and Elias had every week about the agents on the team. Honest. Measured. Objective.

And they were talking about him.

He waited until their voices moved deeper into the suite before he picked up his bag and slipped quietly out the front door.

He sat in his car again. A different feeling this time.

The earlier moment in the parking lot had been private — something he'd whispered to himself, about himself, for himself. This was different. This was someone else's observation, made without his knowledge, because it was simply true from where they were standing.

He's consistent. He listens. He applies.

He drove home slowly, thinking about what it meant to be believed in by people who had seen enough agents come through to know exactly what they were looking at — and who had no reason to say what they'd said except that they meant it.

* * *

By mid-January, something new had settled into his days. Not all at once. Gradually, the way mornings change after the solstice — you don't notice it happening until one afternoon you realize you're driving home with the sun still up.

He no longer felt like he was pretending.

That was the only way he could name it. For months — even through the closings, even through the good weeks, even through the moments that looked from the outside like confidence — there had been a small, persistent voice underneath everything. *You're still figuring it out. You haven't arrived yet. You're just hoping it holds.* The voice wasn't always loud. But it was always there.

By January, it had gone quiet.

He didn't rush into conversations anymore. He didn't answer questions like he was searching for the right answer in real time, triangulating between what he actually knew and what he hoped sounded credible. He didn't freeze when a client looked to him for direction.

He stood a little taller. His voice carried a steadiness that didn't require effort. His calendar was purposeful rather than reactive — built around what mattered, not around what was loudest.

Charlotte noticed during one of their regular reviews.

"You're stepping into your role," she said.

Mason blinked. "My role?"

She nodded. "The role of someone who knows what they're doing." A small smile at the corner of her mouth. "It suits you."

He sat with that for a moment. He wasn't used to receiving something like that — really receiving it, letting it land without deflecting or diminishing it with some version of *I still have a lot to learn.*

He did still have a lot to learn. That was true and would always be true.

But it no longer felt like something to hide behind.

"I'm not becoming a different person," he said finally.

"No," Charlotte agreed. "You're becoming the version you always hoped you'd grow into."

He thought about that on the drive home. He had walked into this office months ago with a full phone and an empty foundation. He had been given tools he didn't yet know how to use and systems he didn't yet trust enough to follow. He had built slowly, awkwardly at first, with more questions than answers and more false starts than he liked to remember.

But he had built.

And what had been built — the habits, the rhythms, the relationships, the disciplines, the willingness to ask for help before he was drowning — all of it had become something he no longer needed to think about consciously. It had become who he was.

Not all at once. Not in a single lesson or a single conversation or a single successfully resolved appraisal.

Gradually. In the accumulated weight of a thousand small decisions made consistently in the right direction.

That was how foundations were built, he realized.

One layer at a time, until you stopped noticing the structure beneath your feet — because you trusted it completely.

He thought about the agents he'd observed over the past year — the ones who were still scrambling, still treating every transaction as a crisis, still confusing noise for work and activity for progress. He didn't look at them with judgment. He'd been that person. He knew what it felt like to hold everything in your head and call it dedication. But he was no longer that person.

And what had changed wasn't the market, or the number of leads, or a single piece of advice that had unlocked everything.

What had changed was him. Slowly, deliberately, one decision at a time.

* * *

FOUNDATION MARKER

Leadership Window

The identity shift is not a single moment — it is an accumulation of small decisions made consistently over time until they no longer require effort. The agent who wonders when they will feel like a real professional is usually already becoming one. The work precedes the feeling. Always.

You should now understand:

- Why identity must grow alongside the business — and how that growth happens gradually, not in a single breakthrough moment
- That the clearest sign of a turning point is the absence of fear, not the presence of certainty
- How being observed by trusted colleagues with quiet confidence is a form of external accountability worth internalizing
- That the gap between who you are and who you're becoming closes through repetition, not inspiration
- Why receiving genuine recognition gracefully — without deflecting it — is itself a form of professional maturity

* * *

CHAPTER 17: Consistency Is Stronger Than the Market

Agents who stay steady don't predict the market. They prepare for it.

* * *

February arrived along the North Carolina coast the way it always did — without consensus.

Cold mornings gave way to afternoons warm enough for shirtsleeves. The ocean was restless. Buyers showed up to appointments in parkas and left looking at houses with their jackets tied around their waists. The real estate market had its own version of this seasonal ambiguity: a mix of clients who were ready now and clients who were "thinking about maybe starting in a few months," which in Mason's experience could mean anywhere between six weeks and never.

It was the kind of season that had unsettled him before.

It didn't anymore.

His routine hadn't changed. Ten warm touchpoints every day — personal, specific, not broadcast. Weekly updates from Maya on active files. Biweekly coaching sessions with Charlotte that felt less like check-ins now and more like strategic conversations between two people thinking about the same business from different angles. Monthly financial reviews where he and Elias looked at the numbers together, honestly, and made adjustments when adjustments were needed.

The routine had become, at some point, invisible. Not because he'd stopped doing it, but because it no longer required effort to start. It was just what mornings looked like. It was just how the week was shaped. The structure had internalized itself — which was, he understood now, exactly what structure was supposed to do. You built it consciously until it became unconscious. And then you could put your attention somewhere more useful.

He noticed, somewhere around the third week of February, that what he felt was not the particular relief of a good month or the familiar low-grade anxiety of a slow one.

What he felt was *steady.*

"You're calmer," Charlotte observed one afternoon during their check-in. "Even when things slow."

Mason thought about it for a moment before answering.

"I don't feel stuck when activity dips anymore," he said. "I just adjust."

Charlotte nodded. That was the word — *adjust.* Not panic. Not redecorate. Not abandon what was working and chase whatever felt urgent. Just look at the inputs, see which lever needed a turn, and turn it.

* * *

Elias explained the mechanics of it in his usual direct way.

"The market doesn't control outcomes," he said. "Inputs do. When you know which levers to pull, volatility loses its power."

They looked at Mason's systems together. Daily conversations: consistent. CRM follow-up: not slipping. Pipeline depth: visible at every stage, no surprises lurking in the back half. Weekly reviews: happening on schedule, guiding adjustments before anything quietly became a problem.

"When listings slow," Elias said, "you increase conversations. When buyers hesitate, you spend more time explaining the process rather than pushing toward urgency. When closings stack, you lean harder on leverage." He paused. "No panic. No scrambling. Just movement."

Mason had heard Charlotte use a phrase earlier in the year — *respond, don't react* — and what Elias was describing was the practical architecture beneath it. The difference between a business that responded and a business that reacted was, at its core, a difference of preparation. If the routine was already built, the response to any shift was already built into it. You didn't need to improvise what to do when activity dipped because the system already told you.

He understood it now not as a concept but as something he was actually doing, every day, without thinking much about it.

* * *

The real test came later in the year.

The late summer market tightened in the way that real estate markets sometimes do — slowly at first, then suddenly, in a way that felt abrupt even though the signs had been there for anyone who had been watching. Rates bounced. Buyers who had been moving with confidence through the summer began to hesitate. Sellers who had been planning to list in September started asking whether to wait. The news cycle found the story and amplified it until it sounded bigger than it was.

Mason had been paying attention all summer. That was the difference he noticed most clearly when the shift arrived. He wasn't caught off guard because he'd been tracking the inputs throughout the warmer months — rate movement, days on market, the tenor of buyer conversations. The tightening wasn't a surprise. It was simply the next thing to respond to.

Mason had clients in every category. A seller who had listed in late September and was watching the market shift beneath the pricing conversation they'd had two months earlier. A buyer who had paused mid-search, nervous about where rates would be in thirty days, asking whether it made more sense to wait.

He understood the instinct to grow quieter in moments like this. Some agents pulled back — stopped posting, slowed their outreach, waited for the market to stabilize before saying anything. The logic was understandable. If things are uncertain, saying less feels safer. Silence doesn't commit you to a position that might turn out to be wrong.

Mason did the opposite.

He leaned harder into warm touches — personal, specific, neighbor-level rather than market-level. He reached out to his homeowner sphere with updates that explained what was actually happening on their specific streets, not the county-wide average numbers that meant nothing to someone trying to decide whether to list a three-bedroom ranch in their particular neighborhood.

He had conversations about the market that were honest, measured, and genuinely useful. Not cheerful spin designed to keep people in motion. Not catastrophizing designed to create urgency. Just clear explanation that helped people understand their specific situation and make better decisions as a result.

This is what's happening. This is what it means for you specifically. Here are the options worth considering.

A buyer who had been frozen for weeks called after one of those conversations and said, simply, "I feel like I can think again."

They were under contract ten days later.

The seller who had been wavering about timing decided, after a forty-minute conversation with Mason that ranged across everything from current absorption rates to her own personal timeline flexibility, to stay the course. They made a small, strategic pricing adjustment and had a new offer within the month. The market hadn't magically improved. But the seller had a clear picture of her situation, a plan she understood, and an agent she trusted to execute it.

His business didn't dip.

It strengthened.

Because consistency wasn't a seasonal tool. It was a survival skill — and, Mason was learning, a growth skill. The agents who stepped back when markets got complicated left room. The agents who stayed present, stayed useful, stayed the same — they were the ones people called when they were finally ready.

There was a line from a conversation with Charlotte that had stayed with him from early in the year: *Your response to every market shift is already built into your system. You just have to trust it enough to keep executing.*

He trusted it now.

The proof was in the numbers. His pipeline hadn't thinned. His conversations hadn't dropped. His clients hadn't disappeared into uncertainty. They'd held on, stayed engaged, made decisions — because he had given them something to hold onto.

"You have something most agents don't," Charlotte told him. She was looking at his metrics with the particular satisfaction of someone watching a thesis prove itself. "You don't wait for the market to give you permission to work."

Mason smiled. "I just kept doing what the systems told me to do."

"Yes," she said. "And that's the whole thing."

She closed her notebook. "The agents who stop when the market gets difficult are the ones who never built the habit when things were easy. You did. And now it's yours whether the market cooperates or not."

Mason thought about February — the cold mornings and warm afternoons and the buyers who were sometimes ready and sometimes not. He thought about the fall tightening, the headlines, the clients who had been uncertain but stayed engaged because he hadn't disappeared.

Consistency wasn't a seasonal tool.

It was the whole thing.

* * *

FOUNDATION MARKER

Leadership Window

Stability is built, not forecasted. Agents who stay steady through market shifts do so not because they predicted correctly, but because they never let prediction replace preparation. The market is always uncertain. The systems are not.

You should now understand:

- Why consistency outperforms market prediction as a long-term business strategy
- How steady inputs — warm touches, follow-up, CRM discipline — create stable outputs regardless of what the market is doing
- That the agent who explains the market clearly becomes the agent people trust when they're finally ready to move
- Why pulling back during market uncertainty is often the most costly decision an agent can make
- How the same behaviors that build momentum in a favorable market protect a business when conditions tighten

* * *

CHAPTER 18: Raising Your Price Point Without Abandoning Anyone

Growth doesn't require leaving people behind. It requires showing up in new rooms while honoring the ones that built you.

* * *

Mason didn't wake up one morning and decide to go luxury.

That wasn't how it worked. He'd watched enough agents attempt that leap — the sudden rebrand, the new headshot with a different wardrobe, the social media presence that shifted overnight to seven-figure listings — and he'd noticed that the ones who repositioned by force rarely landed where they were aiming. They'd moved away from their strengths and into someone else's territory, and the market had a way of noticing.

Charlotte addressed it differently. Practically. During one of their coaching sessions in the late winter, when Mason's average price point was already beginning to shift on its own, she named what was happening.

"You're going to outgrow your average price point," she said. "Not because you decided to chase a different market, but because you served your clients well and word traveled. The people you helped are moving up. Their networks are larger than they were. The referrals coming through are arriving with different budgets."

She was right. He'd noticed it in his pipeline. Buyers arriving through referrals with more purchasing power than his first-year clients had carried. A past client who had introduced him to her sister — a move-up buyer looking in a price range meaningfully above his historical average. A neighbor referral who came with a property priced well above anything Mason had previously represented.

"So, what do I actually do?" he asked.

Charlotte turned to the whiteboard.

She drew a simple set of concentric circles — Mason's existing sphere at the center and a series of expanding rings moving outward.

"You don't abandon the center," she said. "You expand the rings."

She traced the outer edge with her marker.

"Raising your price point isn't about rejecting smaller clients. It's about expanding your reach without shrinking your values."

* * *

They mapped it out together, specifically. Mason would continue serving first-time buyers — the clients who had trusted him when he was new, who had given him the opportunity to practice and refine and earn his confidence through real transactions. He would continue working with modest listings, with long-term nurture clients who were years from their next move but were part of the foundation of his sphere.

These relationships didn't become less valuable because his average price point was rising. They were the reason his reputation existed.

But alongside them, he would add intentional exposure to higher-price opportunities. Not by pretending to expertise he hadn't earned, but by building it deliberately, the way he'd built everything else — through preparation, through showing up, through doing the work that created real knowledge rather than performed confidence.

He began hosting open houses in neighborhoods above his average price point. He studied higher-end listings to understand the expectations that came with them — different marketing standards, different preparation requirements, different client conversations. He attended community events in areas he wanted to grow into, not as a salesperson but as someone genuinely curious about what those neighborhoods were like and who lived in them.

He didn't fake the expertise. He built it.

* * *

The first direct test came in the form of a lunch invitation.

A lender partner Mason had worked with twice — who had sent him two referrals in the fall and was beginning to send more — called with an invitation to join him for lunch with two potential referral sources. An estate attorney. A relocation manager who placed employees relocating to the coastal market.

Months ago, Mason would have found a way to decline.

He would have doubted what he had to offer in a professional setting alongside people who had been working this market longer than he had. He would have worried about being exposed — that they'd ask a question he didn't have the answer to, that the gap between who he was presenting himself as and who he actually was would become visible.

He said yes.

At the lunch, he spoke with a confidence he recognized as earned rather than performed. He talked about market shifts — what was actually happening with inventory and rates, not what the headlines said. He talked about how he managed negotiations, how he protected buyers in competitive situations, how his team's systems ensured nothing fell through the cracks during complex transactions.

The two referral partners listened. They asked real questions. Mason answered them with the kind of specificity that only comes from having actually done the work.

"We'd love to send some clients your way," the estate attorney said, before the check arrived.

Driving back to the office, Mason turned that over in his mind.

Not *we'll keep you in mind.* Not *we appreciate the conversation.* We'd love to send clients your way.

Not because he had impressed them with credentials or authority. Because he had shown them, through the way he talked about his work, that he was someone who understood the whole picture and took it seriously. Someone who could be trusted with a client they cared about.

He was becoming the agent people referred on purpose. Not by accident. Not by luck. By performance, consistently demonstrated in enough conversations and enough situations that it had become something people expected.

* * *

The other piece of the expansion came from a much smaller moment.

A past client named Rachel called one afternoon with what seemed like a simple question.

"Do you offer annual equity reviews?"

Mason paused. He didn't — not yet. He'd thought about it. Charlotte had mentioned the concept in passing as something strong agents built into their long-term client service. But he hadn't created the system around it.

He thought about what Charlotte had said, months earlier: *If a client asks for something reasonable, add it to your system.*

"Yes," he said. "Let's schedule one."

He spent an hour that evening building the template. A home value update based on current comparable sales — specific to Rachel's neighborhood, not a generic range. Neighborhood market trends. A mortgage payoff estimate, so she could see what she'd paid down. Projected equity and what that number might make possible: a move-up purchase, a refinance, a rental investment. A section for questions and future conversations.

Rachel received it three days later. She called within the hour.

"This is incredible," she said. "I didn't expect this."

She sent the summary to three people in her network — not because Mason asked her to, but because it was useful enough that she wanted to share it. Within two weeks, two of those three had reached out to schedule their own reviews.

Mason hadn't launched a campaign. He hadn't advertised a new service. He had listened to a client's question, answered it thoroughly, and built the answer into something he could repeat.

That was the whole model, Charlotte reminded him when he told her.

"Expansion doesn't have to be dramatic," she said. "Most of the time it looks exactly like what you just did. Someone asks for something reasonable. You say yes. You build it so you can do it consistently." She looked at the template he'd printed out. "Your clients grow. Your services should too. But the growth comes from listening to the people already in your world — not from chasing a market you haven't earned yet."

Mason thought about the lender lunch. The estate attorney who had already texted twice. The relocation manager who placed three to five employees into the coastal market every quarter and was now routing them to Mason's cell number.

He thought about Rachel's network, people who had seen the equity review and now knew his name and what he offered.

None of it had required him to become someone else.

It had required him to become more fully himself — more prepared, more confident, more useful — and to show up in rooms he might once have found reasons to avoid.

Growth and integrity, he was learning, moved together. When one was solid, the other followed naturally. The business he was building didn't require him to abandon what had made it worth building in the first place. It asked him to carry those values into every new room he entered.

That, he understood, was what expansion was supposed to feel like.

* * *

FOUNDATION MARKER

Leadership Window

Growth without integrity is not growth. The agent who expands their price point through genuine competence and deepened service finds the new territory welcoming. The agent who chases it through repositioning alone usually discovers the ground is less solid than it appeared from a distance.

You should now understand:

- How price point expansion happens gradually through intentional presence in new environments — not rebranding or reinvention
- Why serving existing clients exceptionally is the foundation for attracting higher-value opportunities
- How adding services in response to client requests creates durable growth without requiring a marketing campaign
- That confidence in professional settings is a product of preparation, not personality
- Why expanding capacity — what you can offer and who you can serve — is different from abandoning the clients who built your business

* * *

CHAPTER 19: Marketing That Supports Relationships

Your best marketing comes from listening well.

* * *

Mason used to think marketing was something he had to keep up with.

Not master. Not deeply understand. Not deploy strategically in a way that reinforced the actual work he was doing.

Just survive.

Everywhere he looked, someone had an opinion about what the right approach was. Post more. Mail more. Boost this listing. Brand that neighborhood. Film a reel. Go live on Tuesday at noon. Use this hashtag. Feature your face on every available surface so people don't forget you exist. The noise was relentless and oddly consistent in its urgency — as if the specific strategy didn't matter as much as the sheer insistence that whatever you were doing, you needed to be doing more of it.

It was overwhelming. And more than overwhelming, it was distracting. Every week brought a new platform that promised to change everything, a new format that guaranteed leads, a new approach that would make everything else obsolete. Mason had spent the early months of his career in a low-grade state of marketing anxiety — perpetually behind on something he didn't fully understand but was constantly told he couldn't afford to neglect.

Elias cut through it in one sentence.

"Marketing is not your job," he said. "Relationships are."

Mason sat with that.

"Then what's marketing for?"

Elias didn't hesitate. "Reinforcing the relationships you're already building. Not replacing them. Not substituting for them. Amplifying the work you're already doing so the right people remember you when they're ready."

* * *

Charlotte expanded the conversation during their next session.

"You're on a team within a brokerage that has already invested heavily in marketing infrastructure," she said. "Brand standards. Listing materials. Email campaigns. Digital ads. Social tools. Postcards. Compliance already handled. All of it is there for you."

Mason had known this, the way you know something without fully using it. He'd assumed he needed to do something additional — something more personal, more original, more distinctly *him* — to stand out from the team's standard offerings.

Charlotte shook her head.

"Use the leverage that's already here," she said. "That's why it exists. Your brokerage has people who specialize in design, messaging, compliance, distribution, and technology. Your job isn't to become all of those people. Your job is to decide what's worth saying and to whom. Then let the specialists handle how it gets executed."

The realization landed the same way the delegation conversation had. This wasn't a concession to what he couldn't do. It was a recognition of where his energy was worth the most. The highest-value work was the work only Mason could do — knowing his clients, understanding their situations, crafting the specific insight that would help them. Everything else had a better home.

* * *

Charlotte asked a question that reset the entire frame.

"If someone receives your marketing, what do they gain?"

That became the filter.

He stopped thinking about content as something produced to maintain visibility and started thinking about it as something offered to provide value. The distinction was small on the surface and enormous in practice — it changed what he created, how specific he made it, and what success looked like when he reviewed it.

For his homeowner sphere, he began sharing neighborhood-specific market updates. Not county-wide averages that felt distant and generic, but the specific absorption rates and pricing shifts for the streets and subdivisions where his past clients lived. He explained what the numbers meant in plain language, connecting data to decision: *Here's what's happening. Here's what it means for someone in your position.*

For buyers in his pipeline, he created content that explained the process in the honest, practical language he used in consultations. What inspections actually revealed and why they rarely killed deals. How to approach a competitive offer situation without panic. What the weeks between contract and closing actually looked like.

For his sphere in general, he moved away from content that was implicitly asking — *use me, refer me, think of me* — and toward content that was simply offering. Stories that demonstrated how he worked. Explanations that made something complicated feel manageable. Invitations to a conversation, not a transaction.

Marketing stopped being noise. It became reinforcement.

* * *

The market videos came out of this shift, and they came out imperfectly.

Mason was not a natural on camera. His first few attempts sat in his phone's draft folder for a week — too polished to feel real, too careful to feel genuine. He'd written out what he wanted to say and then lost the thread the moment he pressed record, the scripted version of himself sounding nothing like the person who sat across from clients in consultations.

He scrapped the ring light. He stopped writing scripts.

He turned on his phone camera in his car or at his desk after a week of market activity, and he simply talked about what he'd seen. A conversation with a seller about pricing that surprised him. What multiple offers were actually like to navigate from his side. Why rates mattered less in some decisions than people thought, and more in others.

No filters. No production. No attempt to perform expertise he'd already earned and didn't need to manufacture.

He just spoke clearly. Calmly. The way he talked to clients who needed help understanding something unfamiliar.

One afternoon, a message arrived from a past client he hadn't spoken to in three months.

I love how you explain things. It makes everything feel less scary.

He read it twice.

Less scary.

He shared it with Charlotte.

She smiled. "That's it," she said. "That's the whole thing."

She reminded him how to measure marketing in a way that was actually useful. Not likes. Not impressions. Not follower counts or engagement rates or any of the metrics that felt important on a dashboard and meant nothing in practice.

Conversations started. Recognition in the community — people who saw him at a neighborhood event and said *I've been following your videos*. Trust built over time, the slow accumulation of someone being consistently present and consistently useful until they became the person who came to mind first when the moment arrived.

"When someone is finally ready," Charlotte said, "your name is already there. They don't have to search. They don't have to ask three people and compare. You're already the answer."

Elias added the last piece.

"Being useful," he said, "will always outperform being loud."

* * *

The CRM guided the decisions more than anything else.

Who hadn't heard from Mason in a while? The answer was right there — contacts flagged for follow-up, dates showing the last meaningful touch. Who was entering a new life phase? The notes he'd kept told him: a client who had mentioned a promotion, a past buyer whose family was growing, a homeowner who had asked a question three months ago about what their equity looked like now.

Marketing followed relationships. Not the other way around.

The goal was never to manufacture urgency or create desire where there wasn't any. It was to stay present and useful, consistently, so that when the moment arrived — when someone's circumstances shifted and the decision to buy or sell moved from abstract to real — Mason was already part of the picture.

He wasn't selling to people.

He was staying connected to them.

And when they were ready, they knew exactly where to turn.

Some weeks the marketing was a video. Some weeks it was a personal text to a past client whose neighborhood had seen something unusual in the data. Some weeks it was an equity review delivered without prompting, sent because the CRM flagged that it had been a year and the market had moved enough to make the update worth sharing.

None of it was loud. None of it performed.

All of it was useful.

And useful, Mason had come to understand, was the most durable thing a person could be in a relationship built on trust. Visibility faded. Relevance held. The agent who showed up with something that mattered, consistently, was the agent people remembered when it was time to make the most important financial decision of their lives.

Marketing, he realized, was simply relationship management at scale. It followed the same rules as every other part of the business: be consistent, be specific, be useful, and let the compounding do the work.

* * *

FOUNDATION MARKER

Leadership Window

Relevance beats visibility. The agent who is remembered as useful — who explained the confusing thing clearly, who sent the update that actually applied, who showed up at the right moment with the right information — will always outlast the agent who is simply seen frequently. Presence is not enough. Presence with purpose is.

You should now understand:

- Why relationship-first marketing produces more durable results than visibility-first marketing
- How to use team and brokerage marketing infrastructure as leverage rather than building everything independently
- What value-based marketing actually looks like — specific, relevant, designed to help rather than to promote
- Why the CRM is your best marketing guide — it tells you who needs what and when, before you have to guess
- How to measure marketing by the conversations it starts and the trust it builds, rather than the impressions it generates

* * *

PART III TRANSITION — FOUNDATION IN PRACTICE

Weight-Bearing Growth

* * *

As Mason's production increased, so did complexity.

More listings. More negotiations. More moving pieces, more conversations requiring his full attention, more clients whose trust he was responsible for carrying through to the other side.

In the past, this would have overwhelmed him. The version of Mason who had walked into Charlotte's office months ago with a full calendar and a fragile foundation would have felt this kind of volume as pure pressure — the sense that he was always one missed call or one dropped thread away from something breaking.

This time, something different happened.

Maya managed timelines and client communication without Mason having to ask. Elias handled listing coordination so smoothly that Mason sometimes forgot he'd handed it over. Lily — steadier now, more confident with every week she spent working with Caroline — was beginning to carry genuine weight in the business. Marketing was reinforcing relationships rather than distracting from them. Metrics were guiding weekly adjustments without panic, the numbers telling him what to look at rather than what to fear.

Mason stayed client-facing and strategic.

The business grew. Mason stayed steady.

He sat with that one evening, reviewing his pipeline at his desk before heading home. He thought about the appraisal that had nearly unraveled a transaction and hadn't. He thought about the delegation conversation that had felt uncomfortable and had turned into something he was genuinely glad he'd done. He thought about the December morning when he'd walked into Charlotte's office and said *I think I need help* — three words that had once felt like defeat and now felt like the most professional thing he'd learned to say.

The structure had held.

Not because nothing difficult had happened. Not because the market had cooperated or every transaction had been smooth. But because when the weight arrived — and it arrived, in different forms, throughout the year — the foundation was underneath it. The systems had carried what they were designed to carry. The people around him had played their roles. And he had shown up the way someone shows up when they know what they're doing and why.

The question had shifted.

He hadn't noticed exactly when it happened. But somewhere between the turning point in January and the fall market that hadn't rattled him and the dinner he'd had with the estate attorney, and the equity review he'd created for Rachel and the market video that had made someone feel *less scared* — somewhere in all of it, the question had changed.

It was no longer: *Can this work?*

It was: *Can this last?*

And behind that, quieter and more important: *What kind of life does it make possible?*

He closed his laptop, gathered his things, and stepped out into the December evening. Somewhere in the dark ahead of him, the water was moving. He could hear it.

Part IV would have the answer.

* * *

PART IV — THE LONG VIEW

Can this last, and what kind of life does it make possible?

* * *

Part I was about pouring a foundation strong enough to remove fragility. Part II framed the business so effort could turn into momentum instead of random wins. Part III tested whether that structure could bear weight without cracking under growth. By the time you reach Part IV, the question shifts. It is no longer, "Can this work?" The question becomes, "Can this last, and what kind of life does it make possible?"

The long view is about realizing that the systems you build do more than stabilize your income — they shape your days, your stress level, your relationships, and your choices. A business that constantly feels urgent will eventually consume everything around it, no matter how profitable it becomes. A business that runs on clear numbers, calm structure, and trusted processes does something quite different. It stops being something you survive and starts being something that supports the way you want to live.

By this point, the frantic energy that once defined the work should feel distant. The swings between panic and euphoria are softer. You know your burn rate. You trust your pipeline. Your CRM tells you who to call. Your calendar reflects priorities instead of chaos. The confidence you feel isn't bravado — it is the quiet steadiness that comes from seeing your business respond predictably to the inputs you control. The foundation did that. The frame did that. The way your business carries weight now is proof.

Part IV is not about adding more layers of complexity. It is about alignment. How your business and your life interact. How boundaries are set and held without apology. How trust deepens over years instead of transactions. How relationships compound like interest, quietly and steadily, until the people in your database feel less like clients and more like community.

This final section also confronts a different kind of risk — not collapse, but complacency. When things are working, it becomes easy to coast. The long view asks you to keep refining without constantly reinventing. It asks you to become the kind of agent people turn to not just for a transaction, but for perspective through multiple chapters of their lives.

Most importantly, Part IV invites you to decide — on purpose — what you want your business to make possible beyond production numbers. Time with people who matter. Margin for health and rest. The ability to say no. The freedom to choose what you pursue next without fear that everything will fall apart if you pause to think.

Those outcomes are not accidents. They are the natural byproduct of a business built with a long view in mind.

What you build determines how you live. This final part of the book is about becoming the kind of agent who treats that sentence as a responsibility, not a slogan.

* * *

CHAPTER 20: Protecting the Foundation

Success carries a quiet danger. Its name is complacency.

* * *

Charlotte had been watching the pattern for twenty years.

Agents worked hard to build something. Systems clicked into place. The pipeline filled. Closings came in clusters. And then, somewhere in the stretch between "this is working" and "this feels easy," the disciplines started to slip. Not all at once. Never all at once. Just slowly — a skipped weekly review here, a warm touch pushed back there, a calendar block that dissolved because nothing was urgent enough to justify protecting it.

"The moment things feel easier," Charlotte told Mason one morning, "is when most agents stop doing the basics. That's when cracks form in the foundation."

She leaned back in her chair and looked at him with the particular patience of someone who had said something important before and watched it not land.

"It's never a dramatic failure," she said. "It's a drift. And by the time you notice the drift, you've lost six months of momentum you can't get back."

Mason had heard this kind of warning before — from Charlotte, from Elias, and from every experienced agent who had lived through the cycle. But now it landed differently. He wasn't hearing it as someone learning the ropes anymore. He was hearing it as someone who had something real to protect.

He nodded slowly. "So, the work doesn't change. Even when business is good."

"Especially when business is good."

She paused to let that breathe.

"The agent who builds discipline when they're struggling is common. The agent who maintains it when they no longer have to have to, that's who outlasts everyone."

Mason thought about all the structures he had built over the past year. The warm touches, the weekly reviews, the pipeline stages, the calendar blocks. None of them felt effortful anymore. They were just how he worked. But Charlotte was right — comfortable was the first step toward complacent if he wasn't paying attention.

He made a decision, sitting there across from her: the discipline wasn't going to loosen when business improved. It was going to deepen. Because the business was worth protecting.

* * *

The test soon came.

Everything hit at once.

Two listings needed final prep — photos scheduled, punch lists still incomplete, staging decisions still pending. A buyer Mason had been working with for three months wanted to make an offer before end of day. A seller was anxious and needed price adjustment guidance before the weekend. Another buyer wanted to resume showings after a two-week pause. Lily had a negotiation question that needed Mason's attention before noon. Maya was managing two closings back-to-back, and the lender on one was slow returning calls. A referral source Mason had been cultivating for months sent a message: *Can you do a quick market update call today?*

He read through the list a second time.

In the old version of his life, this moment would have been the beginning of a spiral. He would have felt the walls moving in. He would have opened his laptop, looked at the accumulation of needs, and started reacting without a plan — calling the wrong person first, double-booking his afternoon, spending energy reassuring people rather than actually resolving their questions, finishing the day somewhere between depleted and behind.

Instead, he opened his calendar.

He looked at his time blocks. He looked at his priorities. He looked at his team.

The listing prep belonged to Elias — Mason sent him a detailed text with the outstanding items and trusted the process completely.

He didn't hover. He didn't check back every twenty minutes. Elias had a system. The system worked.

Maya had the closings handled. Mason checked in with a brief message, "*How are we looking on both files?* — got a clean response and let her work.

The price adjustment was genuinely a ten-minute conversation. The seller needed calm, clear context more than she needed a lengthy strategic session. Mason blocked the time, made the call, walked her through the data, and left her feeling steady instead of scared.

The buyer offer was time-sensitive and legitimately required Mason's full attention for most of the morning. He protected that block.

Lily's negotiation question got fifteen focused minutes in the conference room — not a rushed hallway answer, but a real conversation with enough space to be useful.

The referral source got an honest, respectful response: *I have a call opening Thursday morning. I'd love to connect then.* No apology. No stalling. Just a clear, calm redirection to a time that worked.

By Friday, everything was handled.

Not rushed. Not frantic. Handled.

Mason sat at his desk late that afternoon and thought carefully about what hadn't happened. There was no spiral. No dropped ball. No apology email sent at midnight. No client who felt like they were getting the frazzled version of him. No transaction that slipped because his attention was scattered across too many things at once.

The pressure had been real. The week had been full. But it hadn't cracked anything — because the habits underneath were real too.

He thought about what Charlotte had said months earlier, during the appraisal crisis: *Calm is a sign of readiness, not the absence of pressure.* The same pressure that would have overwhelmed him in January had become manageable in June, not because the circumstances were different, but because the foundation beneath them was.

He hadn't built hacks.

He'd built habits. And habits held strong under pressure.

* * *

Then came the lull.

Late summer arrived with slower showings, quieter mornings, messages that trickled instead of flooded. The market was between waves. The frantic energy of spring had dissolved into something softer, and Mason recognized the feeling from the year before — that dangerous combination of relief and restlessness that made agents either panic or coast. The panickers called Charlotte asking if the market was dying. The coasters leaned back, enjoyed the quiet, and let their pipelines dry up.

Mason did neither.

He used the time.

He spent a morning updating his pipeline — every contact reviewed, every next task refreshed, every category reassessed. Some leads had gone cooler than he'd realized. He made notes and scheduled follow-ups. He pulled up his expense report and reviewed where the money was going with the kind of unhurried attention the busy season never allowed. He found one subscription he was no longer using and cancelled it. He found one area of his marketing spend that wasn't converting and decided to redirect it.

He refined his warm touch templates — tightened the language on a few that had started to feel generic, added personal lines to others based on details he'd gathered and logged over the previous months. He went through his listing checklist and added two steps Elias had mentioned in passing, things that had come up on recent transactions and deserved to be formalized.

He followed up with five long-term nurture leads — people he genuinely liked, people who were months away from being ready, people who needed to be reminded they were cared about even when there was no transaction on the horizon. He organized his equity review schedule for the fall.

He started sketching the first real thoughts about the Coastal Cookout, a client appreciation event he wanted to host.

Charlotte stopped by the office on a Wednesday afternoon and found him at his desk, working quietly, in the way people work when nothing is urgent, and everything still matters.

"What are you working on?" she asked.

"Pipeline updates. Some template work. A few follow-ups."

She tilted her head. "You're not worried about the slower week?"

"Should I be?"

She smiled. "No. But most agents would be by now."

Mason leaned back in his chair. "I'm not waiting for business. I'm maintaining the engine."

Charlotte looked at him for a long moment — not the way she'd looked at him a year ago, when she was still measuring how much he understood. She looked at him the way you look at something that has proven itself.

"You're treating this like a real business," she said.

"Because it is," Mason replied.

And for the first time, he felt that truth in his bones, not just his head. It had moved from something he believed intellectually to something he was living. He was a business owner. Not someday. Right now. Even in the quiet weeks. Especially in the quiet weeks.

* * *

The foundation had held in the storm. It held in the calm, too.

That, Mason understood, was the whole point. Any structure looks strong under ideal conditions. The real test is what happens when pressure arrives — and what happens when it lifts. Whether you maintain discipline when discipline costs something. Whether you maintain it when nothing requires you to. When you could get away with skipping and no one would know and nothing would immediately break.

The answers, it turned out, were the same in both seasons.

You protect the foundation not because you're afraid. You protect it because you've seen what it holds.

* * *

FOUNDATION MARKER

Leadership Window: What you protect determines what lasts. Most agents guard their systems during hard times and abandon them when things feel easy. But the discipline that builds momentum is the same discipline that sustains it. Maintenance is not the absence of leadership — it is leadership at its quietest and most essential.

You should now understand:

- Why consistency matters more as success grows, not less — complacency is a success-season problem
- How drift forms slowly, through small disciplines that slip rather than dramatic failures
- Why refinement beats reinvention — the foundation needs maintenance, not replacement
- How to use slow periods productively, as preparation for the next wave rather than passive waiting
- That the real test of a system is whether you protect it when you could afford to skip it

* * *

CHAPTER 21: Your Mindset Must Expand Before Your Business Can

Your beliefs become your ceiling — until you break them.

* * *

The conversation started with a simple question over coffee.

"How many units do you think you can close this year?"

Mason considered it honestly. He had momentum now. The systems were working. The warm touches were compounding, the pipeline was healthy, the team was running well. He was doing the daily work and staying consistent. By any reasonable measure, things were going well.

"Maybe twenty," he said. "That feels reasonable."

Charlotte set her cup down.

"Why twenty?"

"I don't know," he said. "It feels safe."

She shook her head — not unkindly, but with the kind of directness that had defined every important conversation they'd had.

"Safe is not the goal. Accurate is."

She pulled out a sheet — his activity numbers, his pipeline velocity, his current pace, the data she had been tracking since the beginning of the year. She had done the math.

Projected Units at Current Pace: 32–38.

Mason stared at the page.

"That can't be right."

"It is," Charlotte said matter-of-factly. "You're building momentum. You're using leverage. You're consistent. You're ready."

He felt something flutter in his chest — a complicated mixture of excitement and something that functioned like dread. The number on the page was possible. He could see that. But possible and wanted were different things when wanting something meant risking not getting it.

"What if I really can hit 36?" he said. The question came out quieter than he'd meant it.

"Then we'll plan for it," Charlotte said.

And that was the moment his ceiling lifted. Not because the number changed. Because he stopped protecting himself from the possibility.

* * *

A few weeks later, Charlotte pressed further in a way that was harder to deflect.

"What scares you about hitting 36 units this year?"

They were sitting in her office on a Thursday morning, the kind of coaching session that felt like a conversation until suddenly it didn't. Mason looked at her for a moment before answering. She wasn't asking because she expected him to fail. She was asking because she wanted to see where the resistance lived.

He gave her an honest answer.

"What if I can't keep the pace?" he said. "What if I drop the ball on someone? What if I disappoint a client, I've built a real relationship with? What if volume creates chaos I can't control?"

Charlotte let him finish without interrupting.

"You're not doing this alone," she said. "You have Elias and Maya and systems that exist precisely, so you don't have to hold it all yourself. And more than that — you have discipline. Real discipline, built over twelve months of actual choices. That's why your business is growing. Not because you're hustling harder. Because you're thinking bigger."

She tapped her pen on the notepad.

"Fear isn't a sign you're failing. Fear is a sign you're expanding. The agent who's playing it safe doesn't feel what you're feeling right now. They're not scared because they're not reaching."

Mason took a slow breath.

She was right. He had been so careful not to let himself want too much — as if wanting it made failure worse, as if keeping his expectations low was a form of self-protection. But Charlotte had just named the flaw in that logic. Limitation wasn't safety. It was just a smaller box.

He had outgrown the box.

* * *

He overheard the other conversation by accident.

He was getting coffee in the break room when an agent he recognized — newer to the team, earnest in his effort — sat down in the open office area, phone pressed to his ear, frustration plain in his voice.

"This market is just impossible right now. Nothing's working. I don't know what else to try."

Mason stood at the counter with his cup.

He felt a deep, genuine pang of recognition. He had been that agent — not so long ago, really, if he was honest about the timeline. The frustration in the other agent's voice was real. The exhaustion was real. The sense of effort completely disconnected from results was one of the hardest feelings he had ever sat with for an extended period of time.

But now, standing on the other side of the work, Mason could see something clearly that he couldn't see when he was living it.

It wasn't the market. Not really.

The agent on the phone was working. Mason didn't doubt that. He had seen the man in the office early and late, making calls, running showings. The effort was genuine. But effort without strategy had a ceiling — a low one. Without a lead generation system, without a pipeline review, without warm touches compounding over months, without leverage to free up his attention, without financial clarity to keep him calm between closings, the work was running in circles rather than building on itself.

He was doing activity. He wasn't running a business.

Mason almost went back to his desk. A year ago, he would have. He remembered clearly enough how he'd felt in that season to know that advice from someone who seemed to have figured it out was rarely welcome when you were still in the frustration.

But something stopped him.

He poured a second cup of coffee, walked over, and waited until the agent hung up.

"Rough morning?" Mason asked.

The agent looked up, startled. Then his shoulders dropped. "Rough quarter, honestly. I feel like I'm doing everything and nothing's landing."

Mason sat down across from him. "I know exactly how that feels. I was sitting in that same spot not that long ago." He paused. "Can I make a suggestion?"

The agent nodded.

"Talk to Charlotte. Not about motivation — about structure. She sees things you can't see when you're in the middle of it. And Elias — sit down with him on your numbers. Not because the numbers are bad, but because once you can see them clearly, the decisions get a lot calmer." He took a sip of his coffee. "And Maya. If you're not using her yet, you should be. She'll take half the weight off your plate so you can actually focus on the conversations that move the needle."

The agent studied him for a moment. "Did it actually help? All of that?"

"It changed everything," Mason said. "Not overnight. But the support is there. It's built to work. You just have to be willing to use it."

He stood up, gave the agent a nod, and walked back to his desk.

The moment stayed with him — not because of what he'd said, but because of what it meant that he'd said it. A year ago, he would have kept walking. He wouldn't have known what to offer. Now he did.

He thought about what had actually changed between then and now. Not his personality — he was still the same person. Not his market knowledge — he had been reasonably well-informed from the beginning. Not his care for clients — that had always been genuine. What had changed was the structure underneath. The systems that held the work together so that effort could compound instead of scatter.

The difference between where he'd been and where he was now wasn't talent or luck or a particularly favorable market.

It was that he'd built a real business. And a real business didn't rely on luck to function.

* * *

The coaching session happened on a slow Thursday morning.

Charlotte asked: "What do you see for yourself next year?"

Mason didn't hesitate the way he once would have. He didn't search for the safe answer, the modest one, the one that wouldn't sound arrogant if he missed it.

"I want to double down on listings," he said. "That's where my energy is best used. I want to stay consistent with my numbers — not just during busy season but all year, through the slow months when it would be easy to ease off. And I want to invest more back into the business. Better tools, better systems, something meaningful for the client event. Build on what's working rather than constantly trying something new."

Charlotte listened and nodded slowly.

"That's growth thinking," she said. "That's business-owner thinking."

Mason smiled, a little surprised at how naturally the words had come out — how different this conversation felt from the one at the beginning of the year where he had looked at her projection of 32–38 units and said *that can't be right.*

"I guess I've changed," he said.

Charlotte shook her head.

"You didn't change," she said. "You grew."

He held that distinction for a moment.

Change implied leaving something behind — a shedding, a departure from who you had been. Growth meant carrying everything forward. Every lesson, every hard conversation, every quiet morning of discipline when nobody was watching. Every closing that had felt like a test. Every lull that had felt like a warning. Carrying all of it and adding to it, becoming more of who he already was rather than someone different.

His beliefs had once been his ceiling.

Now they were his floor.

* * *

He thought about the agent in the break room for a long time after that day.

Not with judgment — he had genuinely been that agent, and he knew exactly how it felt. But with something that functioned like gratitude: that Charlotte had come along when she had, that Elias had been willing to start with math instead of motivation, that the systems had been built and that he had been willing to stay inside them long enough to feel them work.

The difference between activity and strategy wasn't talent. It wasn't market knowledge or hustle or even care for clients. All those things the other agent had. The difference was the structure underneath — the architecture of a business that directed effort instead of scattering it.

Mason had heard Charlotte say it in their very first meeting: *This team wasn't built to replace effort. It was built to replace guesswork.* He had nodded politely that morning without fully understanding what she meant. Now he knew. The guesswork had been exhausting. It had consumed the same energy as the work itself, leaving nothing for the thing that actually mattered: being fully present with the people he was trying to serve.

The structure had freed him. Not from effort. From confusion.

And that, he realized, was the whole argument for building the foundation in the first place.

* * *

FOUNDATION MARKER

Leadership Window: Mindset shifts happen quietly and then all at once. The beliefs that feel like honesty — "I can probably close twenty units" — are often just fear wearing reasonable clothes. A good mentor doesn't celebrate the safe number. They show you what the data actually says and invite you to decide whether you're willing to match it. Belief is not a personality trait. It is a choice, made daily.

You should now understand:

- Why mindset limits precede business limits — and how to identify where your ceiling actually lives
- How fear of success operates differently from fear of failure, and why both require the same response: forward motion
- The difference between activity and strategy, and why effort without structure has a hard ceiling
- How shifting from employee thinking to owner thinking changes what you plan for, not just what you hope for
- That growth is not change — it is the accumulation and deepening of what you've already built, carried forward with intention

* * *

CHAPTER 22: Becoming the Agent People Trust

Trust is not built by grand gestures. It is built by consistent, quiet presence.

* * *

Trust arrived without announcing itself.

That was the first thing Mason noticed. He had imagined, somewhere in the back of his mind, that he would feel it arrive — some clear moment of recognition, a before and after. He had thought it would feel like an achievement, something that happened once you crossed a threshold of production or experience or reputation.

But that wasn't how it worked.

It came in small moments, easy to miss if he hadn't been paying attention.

* * *

One afternoon in August, his phone buzzed with a voicemail. He recognized the name — a past client named Patricia, a retired teacher who had sold her home of twenty-two years earlier in the year and downsized to a smaller cottage near the water. The transaction had been emotionally complicated. Her home was where she had raised her children, hosted holidays, grieved losses, made memories that didn't fit into MLS categories. She had second-guessed the decision multiple times before closing, and Mason had been patient through every delay, every early morning call, every moment when she needed someone to sit with the uncertainty rather than push her through it.

He pressed play.

"Hey Mason, a coworker of mine is thinking of buying down here. I told her you're the only agent I'd trust. Expect her call."

The only agent I'd trust.

He set the phone down and let those words settle.

He remembered the early months — the uncertainty, the constant feeling that he was one mistake away from everything unraveling. He had been so focused on proving himself, on not dropping the ball, on doing everything right so nothing went wrong. He hadn't been thinking about trust. He'd been thinking about survival.

But Patricia wasn't calling because she needed something from him. She was calling because she wanted to give something — her confidence in him — to someone she cared about. She had become his advocate not because he'd been impressive, but because he'd been present. Because through the hardest moments of the transaction, he had stayed steady when she couldn't.

He earned trust by becoming trustworthy. Not by trying to be trusted.

* * *

A text came from an unknown number.

Hi Mason, three different people told me you're the agent to call. Can we meet?

Three different people.

Mason read it twice, then set his phone down on the desk and looked at the ceiling for a moment.

He had imagined this in the early months — word-of-mouth doing the work, people calling instead of him chasing, the compounding of a reputation built over time. He had imagined it would feel triumphant. Instead, it felt quiet and solid, like something that had always been true finally becoming visible.

When they met — a woman named Rachel, early forties, relocating from Charlotte with her husband and two daughters, serious about finding the right home before a school year started — she said it plainly.

"Everyone I talked to said you're calm, organized, and actually listen. I need that."

Calm. Organized. Listener.

Mason sat with those three words after the consultation. They were the three things he had fought hardest to become — not skills, exactly, but capacities. Things that required systems to support them. A pipeline that wasn't overwhelmed, so he didn't rush conversations.

A calendar that wasn't chaotic so he could stay present. A CRM that held the details, so his mind was free.

The trust Rachel was extending to him wasn't about his sales technique. It was about what kind of presence he had become when his business was running well enough that he could afford to be fully there.

* * *

One warm September morning, he arrived at a listing appointment to find the sellers tense and short with each other. They had been trying to prepare the home themselves for two weeks — the kind of effort that sounds reasonable and becomes exhausting. The fatigue had settled into the house like weather.

Mason walked in with steady energy.

"Let's slow down," he said gently. "We're going to take this one step at a time."

He walked them through the prep timeline, the punch list, the vendor schedule, the staging priorities. He told them what mattered — the things that would show in photos, the things buyers would notice at first showing — and what didn't: the back of the linen closet, the garage shelving, the things that lived in anxiety more than in reality.

He had done this enough times now that the calm wasn't a performance. It was genuine. He knew the process. He trusted it. And that certainty, transmitted quietly through his manner and his words, gave the sellers something to stand on when they couldn't find their footing themselves.

Their shoulders relaxed. Their breathing steadied. They stopped interrupting each other.

"Thank you," the wife said. "We needed someone calm."

Mason smiled. "That's part of the job."

Driving home along the coast that evening, windows down, he thought about that sentence. It was true — not as a marketing claim but as a description of what his presence had become. The value he provided wasn't just knowledge or skill anymore. It was steadiness.

His calmness had become a resource for the people he served, something they drew on when their own reserves ran low.

He hadn't planned for that. It was what a foundation, consistently maintained, eventually made possible.

* * *

Shortly after, a message came from a past client named Diane — a nurse who had bought a townhouse almost two years earlier. No transaction in progress. No question about the market. No request of any kind.

Hey Mason, I don't need anything — I just wanted to say I appreciate how you always check in. It means more than you know.

She didn't want a CMA. She didn't want to buy or sell. She simply felt seen.

Mason thought about the warm touches that had produced that message. The birthday note he sent in March. The equity update in July — a brief, personalized summary of what her townhouse was likely worth now, with a note that she was under no obligation to do anything with the information. The quick text after a neighborhood event she'd mentioned, just to ask if she'd made it.

None of those touches took more than five minutes. But together, over months, they had become something. A relationship that felt like more than a transaction because it was more than a transaction.

He thought about what Elias had said early in the year, talking about the CRM: *When your system is working properly, it tells you exactly what to do each day. You're not relying on memory. You're following a plan.* That plan — ten warm touches a day, every next task assigned, every detail logged — had quietly built the relationships that now built his business.

Loyalty, he understood now, wasn't built by grand gestures. It was built through presence. Checking in. Showing up. Remembering. Caring. Without an agenda. Without a transaction in mind. Just because the relationship was worth maintaining.

Those simple, unremarkable actions were the backbone of everything.

* * *

A warm referral called in October and said something that stayed with Mason for a long time.

"I feel like I already know you. People talk about you like you're part of their family."

Mason laughed. "I just stay connected. That's all."

But as he said it, he knew it wasn't *all*. It was ten warm touches a day, written in his notebook each morning before anything else. It was clear communication at every stage of every transaction, so clients never had to wonder what was happening or whether they were forgotten. It was equity reviews done without being asked, because he had set the reminder and kept the promise. It was thoughtful notes timed to things he'd learned and logged — a promotion, a move, a school start, a loss — because people remembered who remembered them.

Consistency had done something marketing never could.

It had made him familiar. Trusted. Known. Top of mind without ever needing to be loud about it.

Charlotte had said it to him early in the year — in one of their first conversations about the foundation, before he fully understood what she meant.

When you don't need the deal, clients feel safer making decisions.

He understood it completely now.

When his pipeline was healthy, he could let a buyer take the time they needed without feeling the financial pressure of the month bearing down on the conversation. When his numbers were known and his burn rate was covered, a slow week was a lull rather than a crisis. When his systems were running, he could stay fully present with a client rather than silently calculating what the commission would mean.

People could feel all of that. They didn't always name it. They called it calm, or organized, or trustworthy. But what they were actually describing was an agent whose business was stable enough that every client could have his full attention, not the version of him rationing focus across a dozen simultaneous urgencies.

The foundation had made trust possible.

The consistency had made it real.

* * *

FOUNDATION MARKER

Leadership Window: Trust is the long game's dividend. It cannot be rushed, manufactured, or earned in a single impressive transaction. It accumulates through the repetition of simple actions done without fanfare — a check-in call, a remembered detail, a response that doesn't feel desperate. When you stop needing the deal, clients begin to need you. That inversion is the mark of a mature business.

You should now understand:

- Why trust grows when urgency fades — and what systems and pipeline health are required to make that possible
- How consistent, unremarkable actions create a reputation that marketing never can
- Why presence is a professional skill that must be built and maintained, not assumed
- How relationship stewardship differs from lead generation — and why it compounds differently over time
- That the attributes clients use to describe a trusted agent — calm, organized, listener — are structural outcomes, not personality traits

* * *

CHAPTER 23: Leading Others Up

Leadership happens in quiet moments when you help someone else find the way.

* * *

The first thing Mason noticed about Lily as a mentee was that she hadn't asked to be one.

Neither had he asked to become a mentor.

It just happened the way most things happened in real estate when you were doing the work correctly: through proximity, through consistency, through showing up the same way every single day until the people around you began to absorb it. Lily had watched him handle consultations and navigate hard conversations and stay calm during the weeks when everything landed at once. She had paid attention. And somewhere along the way, without either of them naming it, the watching had turned into learning.

He understood later that this was how the best mentorship usually worked. Not through formal programs or structured curricula — though those had their place — but through example, made available to someone ready to learn from it.

* * *

One morning, Lily appeared at Mason's desk clutching her notebook.

"I wanted to update you on Caroline," she said.

Caroline was the buyer Mason had handed to Lily several months earlier — a deliberate choice, made after Mason recognized that his schedule didn't have room to give her the full, unhurried attention a first-time buyer deserved. Lily had been nervous when Mason made the introduction. She had called him twice that first week to talk through strategy, her voice carrying the particular anxious energy of someone trying to do well at something that mattered.

"We toured three homes yesterday," Lily said now, her shoulders relaxed, her voice easy. "She's narrowing in on her top two. She has a clear sense of what matters to her."

Mason looked up. "How's she feeling?"

"Good, I think. She trusts the process." Lily paused. "I've been doing it the way you do it — patient, clear, honest. Walking her through each step before she has to make a decision. Not rushing her."

Her sincerity stopped Mason for a moment.

He hadn't been trying to teach Lily a particular method. He'd just been working — doing the buyer consultation the way he'd learned it, following up the way the CRM reminded him to, explaining the process the way Charlotte had once explained it to him. But Lily had been watching. She had picked up not just the tactics but the philosophy underneath them: that the client's timeline mattered more than his. That clarity served people better than enthusiasm. That an agent who listened more than he spoke earned a different kind of trust.

He was doing the work. The impact reached further than he realized.

"You're doing great," he said. And he meant it.

* * *

Then came the morning Lily burst into the office.

"Mason! Caroline's under contract!"

He stood up from his desk.

"That's incredible." He looked at her face — beaming, a little breathless, holding herself with a confidence that was new. "How do you feel?"

"Honestly?" She paused, savoring the answer. "Confident. And ready for more."

She hesitated before adding something quieter: "And thank you. For trusting me with her."

"You earned it," Mason said. "I just offered the opportunity."

He meant it exactly. He hadn't done anything particularly skillful in handing Caroline to Lily. He had simply looked at the situation honestly: Lily was capable, Caroline needed consistent attention through a slower decision-making process, and Mason had other places where his energy would serve better. It was a practical decision. A business decision.

But watching Lily standing there with her quiet pride, Mason understood that the practical decision had also been a meaningful one. He had given her something real to grow into. Not a favor. A responsibility. And she had met it.

* * *

Then came the afternoon she appeared in the doorway of the conference room, looking anxious.

"I think I'm losing a buyer," she said.

He gestured for her to come in and close the door. She sat across from him and set her notebook on the table.

"Walk me through what happened."

She did — carefully, methodically, the way people recount a situation when they're trying to understand it at the same time, they're describing it. Her buyer couple had gone quiet after a showing that had seemed to go well. They'd been enthusiastic during the tour and then, somehow, the energy had shifted. She had tried to reach out twice. The response was cooler than before. She could feel them slipping.

"They're confused about next steps," she said. "They're second-guessing the whole process. I've tried to reassure them, but it doesn't seem to be helping."

Mason listened without interrupting.

When she finished, he let a beat of silence sit before he spoke.

"What do you think they actually need right now?"

Lily considered it. "Reassurance?"

"Clarity," Mason said. "Not comfort. There's a difference, and it matters." He leaned forward. "Reassurance tells people it's going to be okay, but it doesn't tell them anything new. Clarity tells them exactly where they are in the process, what's coming next, and what decisions are still ahead. When buyers go quiet, it's almost always because the path forward has gotten fuzzy. Walk them through the buyer journey again — starting from right where they are, all the way to closing. Remind them what decisions are still ahead. Show them the timeline. Reset expectations."

Lily exhaled slowly.

"That's so simple. Why didn't I think of that?"

"You were in the emotion of it," Mason said. "Clarity comes from stepping back. You can't see the map clearly when you're holding it against your face."

She smiled — grateful in the way that good mentorship earns. Not gratitude for being rescued, but for being given a tool and trusted to use it.

"You're really good at this," she said.

Mason felt something warm in his chest that wasn't quite pride. It was steadier than that. More like purpose — the feeling of having something worth passing along and finding that it passed well.

* * *

A month later, Lily knocked on Mason's office door.

"Do you have a second?"

"Of course."

She settled into the chair across from him and took a breath.

"I want to take on more," she said. "I've learned a lot over the past few months, and I feel ready to grow. If you ever have buyer leads, you'd trust me with — warm ones, ones where I can really do the work — I'd like the responsibility."

She said it directly. No hedging. No over-qualification.

Mason nodded and felt a quiet satisfaction at hearing her ask that way.

He had a warm buyer lead he'd been nurturing for several weeks — a couple buying their first home, both in their late twenties, who needed patient guidance through a process that felt overwhelming to them. They asked a lot of questions. They needed answers explained more than once. They wanted someone who would take their uncertainty seriously rather than trying to move past it.

In an earlier season, Mason would have handled this lead himself. Now he recognized that Lily was genuinely better suited for it — her natural warmth, her patience with the anxious question, her instinct for slowing down instead of pushing forward. Passing the lead to her wasn't stepping back. It was placing it well.

"This one," he said, pulling up the contact in the CRM. "They're great people. They just need someone who will explain everything twice without making them feel like they're asking too much."

Lily's face lit up. "That's my favorite kind of client."

"I know," Mason said.

* * *

A few days later, she knocked again.

"I wanted to tell you — I'm under contract with the buyer you gave me."

Mason stood.

"That's amazing. How did it feel?"

"Empowering," she said. "Thank you for trusting me."

He felt a swell of something that he recognized, after a moment, as the same feeling Charlotte had described once — the feeling of watching the foundation hold under someone else's weight. Of knowing that what he had built wasn't just for him.

Lily wasn't working his system. She was working the same principles — the same clarity-over-comfort instinct, the same patient follow-through, the same commitment to guiding rather than pushing. She had made them her own. And they were working for her the way they had worked for him.

The foundation was transferable.

It worked for anyone willing to apply it.

Watching someone else rise felt just as meaningful as rising himself.

Maybe more.

* * *

FOUNDATION MARKER

Leadership Window: You do not have to intend to lead in order to lead. Presence, consistency, and craft — demonstrated quietly over time — become the standard others rise toward. The best mentorship is not a curriculum. It is an example, made available to someone ready to learn from it. When you trust someone with real work, you give them more than a task. You give them evidence of what they're capable of.

You should now understand:

- When mentoring is appropriate — and how it emerges naturally from doing excellent work consistently
- How to delegate as development, not just as efficiency — giving people real work that grows them
- Why clarity is a leadership tool, and how it serves differently than comfort or reassurance
- That the foundation is transferable — the same systems and principles work for anyone willing to apply them
- That leadership as legacy is built in quiet moments, through the choice to share what you know rather than protect it

* * *

CHAPTER 24: The Numbers Tell the Story

When you understand the numbers, they start working for you.

* * *

The mid-year review happened on a Tuesday morning in June.

Charlotte had the numbers organized before Mason arrived — pulled from the CRM, from the transaction tracking sheet, from the pipeline stages he reviewed each week. She had done this kind of review many times, with many agents, and she knew how to read the difference between an agent who had worked hard and got lucky and an agent who had built something that ran on inputs he controlled.

She walked Mason through the sheet with the unhurried pace of someone who had learned that numbers, when you knew how to read them, were nothing to brace for.

18 closed. 5 under contract. 8 active. 11 warm leads in nurture. On pace for 36 units.

Charlotte leaned back.

"You're exactly where you planned to be," she said. "And do you know why?"

Mason considered it genuinely, turning the question over before answering.

"Warm touches. Systems. Support. Consistency."

"Yes," Charlotte said. "But more than that." She tapped the tracking sheet. "You're consistent even when business is good. Most agents stop when the pipeline fills. They ease off because it feels earned. They take a breath, coast for a few weeks, and lose the compounding effect they'd been building for months." She looked at him steadily. "You don't do that."

She let that land.

"That's the difference between agents who have a good year and agents who build a business they can repeat."

Mason studied the numbers. A year ago, seeing figures like these on a page would have felt as though they belonged to someone else's story — someone further along, someone with more experience, more connections, more years in the market. Now they felt like his own. Because they were. Each line on that sheet connected to a specific choice: a morning he opened his notebook instead of his phone. A follow-up call he made when he didn't feel like making it. A referral he had earned by staying in touch for eight months before anything was ready to move.

He wasn't slowing down.

He was building up.

* * *

Charlotte had updated the P&L and she didn't build slowly toward the number. She said it directly.

"You're officially on track to net six figures this year."

Mason stared at the screen.

"I — I did it?"

"You built it," Charlotte corrected.

The correction mattered. He heard it.

They went through the details together — marketing expenses, tax reserves, operational costs, net profit projections for Quarter 3 and Q Quarter 4. Mason expected to feel shocked. He had imagined this moment during slow mornings and drives along the coast, had thought about what it would feel like to have that number confirmed. He had expected something dramatic. A rush. A moment he'd want to mark.

Instead, he felt grounded.

Calm, in the way that truth is calming when you already suspected it and just needed someone to confirm it out loud.

This wasn't luck. It wasn't a fluke or a fortunate stretch of the market or a single deal that had changed the year's trajectory. It was the result of choices made daily, most of them unremarkable in isolation. Ten warm touches. Pipeline review. Weekly metrics. Expenses tracked. Budget maintained. None of it was exciting. All of it had compounded.

For the first time, he saw the full chain clearly. The CRM discipline he had maintained since Maya first showed him how to use it properly — that had led to the warm follow-ups that had led to the referrals that had led to the closings that were now reflecting back at him on a P&L. The time blocking that Charlotte had introduced, the ideal week that Elias had helped him build — those had created the space for the buyer consultations and listing appointments and proactive touches that had filled the pipeline that was now producing the results on the screen.

He wasn't just making money.

He was running a business.

"This wasn't luck," Mason said.

"No," Charlotte agreed. "This was structure."

* * *

The final review of the year came in late September.

Charlotte pulled Mason into her office on a gray Thursday afternoon — the kind of fall day along the coast where the light goes low early and the air has the particular weight of a season closing. She opened her laptop and turned the screen toward him.

"You're on pace for 34 to 37 units," she said. "If your December closings all hit, you'll reach your net goal."

Mason exhaled slowly.

"I can't believe it."

Charlotte smiled — not the warm, reassuring smile of a mentor trying to make someone feel better, but the quiet, satisfied smile of someone watching a plan prove itself over time.

"This is why we plan," she said. "Planning protects you from accidental success. It turns success into something you can repeat."

She paused.

"Do you understand the difference?"

Mason thought about that carefully. Accidental success — a strong year built on momentum and favorable timing and the particular alchemy of factors that sometimes align. Something to be grateful for and then quietly nervous about repeating because you weren't sure what you had done to produce it. Versus sustainable success — the same production, built on inputs he understood and controlled, inputs he could return to deliberately the following year and the year after that.

He understood the difference completely.

"I used to think a good year meant I was good," he said. "Now I think a good year means the system is good. And I can rebuild the system any time."

Charlotte tilted her head, as if the phrasing had surprised her.

"That's exactly right," she said.

They reviewed the fourth-quarter goals together. The Coastal Cookout timeline. The final wave of follow-ups before the event. Financial projections for Q1 of the coming year. Positioning.

Mason walked out of that meeting feeling the same way he had walked out of his very first financial review with Elias — not excited, exactly, but grounded. Clear. Like someone who had looked at the math and found that it made sense.

He stood in the hallway for a moment before going back to his desk.

He thought about all the agents he knew who treated their financial picture as something that existed outside their control — something that arrived each month like weather, to be received and reacted to rather than shaped. He had been that agent. He had looked at his bank account to understand how the business was doing, rather than looking at his numbers to understand what the business needed.

The shift from one to the other was the shift from surviving to building.

A P&L was not a verdict. It was a tool. A referral rate was not a measure of likability. It was a diagnostic. Pipeline strength was not a reflection of luck. It was a reflection of inputs — touchpoints made, consultations booked, follow-ups completed, relationships maintained.

When you understood that, the numbers stopped being something you braced for. They became something you worked with. Something you adjusted toward. Something that, over the course of a year, told a story with a clear beginning, middle, and end.

The story his numbers were telling right now was the story of a business that had been built correctly.

He went back to his desk and started planning Q1.

He thought back to sitting across from Elias at that desk while the commission breakdown appeared on paper for the first time. The P&L categories. The Profit First framework. The first-time money had felt like something he could direct rather than something that happened to him.

The story had come full circle.

The numbers didn't lie. They also didn't panic. They didn't catastrophize or amplify doubt or keep score in ways that couldn't be answered. They simply told the truth — and the truth, when you were willing to look at it honestly, it turned out to be something you could work with.

* * *

FOUNDATION MARKER

Leadership Window: Financial reviews are not report cards. They are conversations between you and your business — a chance to understand what your discipline is producing and what still needs attention. The agent who reviews their numbers quarterly builds a confidence the one who avoids them never finds. Numbers seen regularly lose their power to frighten. They become tools.

You should now understand:

- How to read a mid-year review as a diagnostic, not a judgment — numbers reveal what to adjust, not what to fear
- Why planning turns success from an accident into a repeatable result
- How each financial review deepens financial confidence by connecting daily habits to long-term outcomes
- That the connection between warm touches and closings becomes visible only through consistent tracking over time
- How the P&L story that began in Chapter 4 compounds across a full year into something recognizable and repeatable

* * *

CHAPTER 25: The Coastal Cookout

Your community grows when you give without asking for anything in return.

* * *

The idea had been sitting in his mind since July.

During the lull — those quieter mornings when he had been updating his pipeline and refining his templates and thinking about the fall — Mason had started thinking about the people in his database. Not abstractly, the way you think about a list. Specifically. By name.

Patricia, who had trusted him with the sale of her twenty-two-year home. The young couple from Wilmington who had texted him a photo of their finished nursery, just because they thought he'd want to see it. The retired school principal who sent him referrals regularly because, as he had said with characteristic bluntness, *You're the only agent I've worked with who actually calls back.* The lender who had stayed late on a Friday to push through a complicated approval because she knew Mason wouldn't have called unless it genuinely mattered. Rachel, who had found him through three different referrals and thanked him afterward for making the process less scary than she'd feared.

These people had made his business possible. Not just by giving him transactions — though they had done that. By trusting him with something more personal. Their decisions. Their uncertainty. The chapters of their lives that intersected with real estate and all the complexity that real estate carried.

He wanted to say thank you.

Not in a newsletter. Not with a branded holiday card or a fridge magnet with his headshot. In person. In a way that felt like something.

* * *

He mentioned it to Charlotte over coffee.

"I want to do something for the people who built this business," he said. "Not a marketing event. A celebration. A way to show my clients that I appreciate them."

Charlotte looked at him with the particular attention she gave to things that interested her.

"What's the difference?" she asked.

Mason thought about it. "Marketing is about what comes next — another transaction, another referral, keeping the name out there. This is about what already happened. The relationships that are already real. I want those people to feel that I know what they gave me. I want them to feel celebrated."

Charlotte nodded slowly. "Then do it right."

* * *

He called it the Coastal Cookout.

The planning took two months and required the same discipline as anything else worth doing well.

He wrote personal notes — not form letters with a name inserted at the top, but actual notes that referenced something specific from each relationship.

He found all of it in his CRM, logged in real time over the past year. The details he had entered not because they were transactionally useful but because they were human — the kind of thing you wrote down because you wanted to remember it.

He sent video messages to his referral partners — short, face-to-camera, filmed during lunch rather than produced into something that would feel corporate. The lender. The home inspector he had come to trust. Two agents in other markets who send him business regularly. *I'm hosting something this fall for the people who've made this year what it was. I'd really love to have you there.*

He followed up on the RSVPs personally. He confirmed details twice. He arranged the catering through a local restaurant rather than a corporate caterer because the food was better and because it felt more like the coast and less like a conference.

"This isn't just a thank-you," he told Charlotte one afternoon. "It's a celebration of the relationships that built my business."

Charlotte smiled. "That's the heart of it."

He wasn't throwing an event. He was nurturing a community.

* * *

The day of the Coastal Cookout arrived on a Saturday in late October.

The park sat a few blocks from the waterfront — open grass, old oaks, picnic tables scattered between them in the generous way of parks that predate landscaping trends. Mason had arrived early to help Elias with the setup: folding tables draped in navy cloth, string lights strung between the oaks, coolers packed and organized. There was food — good food, the kind you eat in actual conversation rather than moving past politely — and a playlist he had built himself over several evenings, songs that felt like the coast.

By noon, the park was alive.

A warm breeze came off the water. The sky was the particular shade of blue that coastal October occasionally delivers — deep and clear, generous with afternoon light. The kind of day that makes you feel like you belong somewhere.

Patricia arrived with her sister, and she hugged Mason the way people hug someone they consider family — no awkwardness, no performative warmth, just genuine affection. The young couple from Wilmington came with their baby. The retired principal pumped Mason's hand and said, loudly enough for the people nearby to hear, "Best real estate decision I ever made was working with this guy."

Mason laughed. He didn't have a practiced response to that.

Lily moved through the crowd with the ease of someone who genuinely enjoyed people — stopping to chat, connecting names to faces she had heard Mason mention, asking questions that showed she had been paying attention to the stories behind the names. She was in her element. The clients responded to her immediately.

Maya worked the guest table near the entrance with her characteristic calm efficiency, checking names, handing out name tags, directing people toward the food with the quiet competence that made every interaction feel effortless rather than managed. She had offered to help before Mason even asked.

Elias circulated near the setup area, making sure the coolers stayed stocked and the folding chairs were in the right configuration. He caught Mason's eye at one point and gave a small, satisfied nod — the kind of acknowledgment shared between people who have built something together and are watching it work.

Charlotte sat in the shade of the largest oak tree, a glass of lemonade in her hand, watching.

Mason moved through the crowd and felt something he had not felt before — or had not let himself feel, maybe. Not the accomplishment of a strong year or the relief of an event going well. Something deeper and quieter than either of those.

He felt like he belonged here.

Not like a host managing an event. Like someone whose life had grown to include this — this particular group of people, on this particular day, in this particular place. The community had formed not because he had engineered it, but because he had been consistent enough, and present enough, and real enough that people had gathered around it.

He wasn't standing in the middle of a marketing event.

He was standing in the middle of his life's work.

Later, after the informal remarks he kept intentionally short — because this wasn't about him giving a speech, it was about people enjoying each other — he stood near the edge of the park and just watched. Conversations forming and reforming as the afternoon moved. Laughter bouncing between the oak trees. The particular quality of light that coastal fall produces, low and warm and gold at the edges.

People weren't there for free food.

They were there because they felt connected. Seen. Appreciated.

Because Mason had shown up for them consistently, long before there was any event to invite them to.

* * *

That was the whole book, Mason thought.

Not in a chapter. Not in a conversation with Charlotte. In a park on a Saturday afternoon, watching the people his foundation had made possible.

One warm touch at a time.

One year of showing up.

A community he hadn't planned to build — just the natural result of choosing, every day, to care about the people in his database as people rather than transactions.

* * *

FOUNDATION MARKER

Leadership Window: Client appreciation is not a marketing strategy. It is the external expression of an internal truth: that the relationships in your database are the most valuable asset your business holds. When you celebrate without asking for anything in return, people feel the difference between an agent who values them and one who values what they represent. That difference is everything.

You should now understand:

- Why client events deepen loyalty in ways that campaigns and content cannot replicate
- How to plan an appreciation event that feels personal rather than promotional — and why the difference matters
- That community is built through consistent presence over time; the event is simply where it becomes visible
- How the full team — operations, coordination, leadership — shows up in the client experience at every level
- That giving without asking is not a strategy or a tactic. It is the natural expression of a business built around genuine relationships

* * *

CHAPTER 26: What the Foundation Makes Possible

The strongest structures are invisible. You only notice them when they fail.

* * *

Charlotte found him packing up chairs.

The cookout had wound down slowly the way good things do — conversations extending past the food, past the afternoon light, into the soft cooling air of early evening until it was just a handful of people standing between the oaks, reluctant to let the day end. Elias had loaded the tables into his truck. Maya had collected the last of the name tags and said her goodbyes with the quiet warmth she brought to everything. Lily had headed out with a few clients who were walking toward the waterfront.

Mason was folding the last of the chairs, alone with the string lights and the fading October light, when he heard Charlotte's footsteps on the grass.

"You did it," she said quietly.

He straightened up and looked at her. She wasn't smiling the way she smiled when something went well. She was smiling the way she smiled when something was true.

"I really did," he said.

She stood beside him for a moment, looking at the park — the empty tables, the scattered leaves, the lights still strung between the oaks.

"You didn't just hit 36 units," she said. "You built a business you can repeat. Sustain. Grow. Share."

Mason looked out at the park.

"I know," he said. And for the first time, knowing it didn't feel like relief. It felt like a starting point.

"I'm ready for whatever comes next."

Charlotte looked at him — the same way she had looked at him a year ago in her office, when she had said *you're doing activity, not building* — but with everything reversed.

"I know you are," she said.

Because he wasn't just a real estate agent anymore.

He was a professional. A leader. A business owner.

* * *

The next morning, Mason woke before his alarm.

The sky outside the window was the gray-pink of early coastal morning — not quite dawn, not quite dark, the particular light that belongs to the hour before the day commits to itself. He dressed quietly and went downstairs, brewed coffee in the silence, and sat at the kitchen table.

He opened his notebook.

He wrote his warm touches for the day.

Ten names. Ten relationships. Ten opportunities.

Not leads. Not prospects. Not contacts in a funnel. People — people whose lives he had been invited into, whose decisions he had helped navigate, whose trust he had earned one consistent day at a time.

He wrote them slowly, pausing after each name to let something specific surface. Patricia, and the small sunlit kitchen she had stood in and said, "*I think this might be it.* Rachel, who had found him through three referrals and thanked him for making everything feel less overwhelming. The Wilmington couple and their toddler who had run toward the other children without hesitation. The principal whose handshake still felt warm in memory.

When he finished, he capped the pen and looked at the page.

His journey wasn't ending.

It was compounding.

Growing. Strengthening. Expanding. One consistent action at a time.

* * *

He sat with his coffee and thought about the year.

He thought about the morning Charlotte had called him into her office — the first real conversation, the one that had started everything. *You're doing activity. That's not the same thing.* He had walked out uncertain and a little stung. He thought he had been building something. It turned out he had been staying busy, which is different in the same way that a sprint is different from a pace you can sustain for years.

He thought about Elias at the whiteboard, drawing out the burn rate in two clean columns. The relief of seeing the number on paper, the way clarity had replaced the ambient dread that had lived in the space where the unknown had been. He thought about Maya in the CRM, pointing to a contact without a next task: *No next task. That's how people get lost.*

He thought about the appraisal that came in low. The late December busy season that he had navigated without cracking. The quiet lull in July when he had refined his templates instead of waiting for the phone to ring. The morning he had opened his calendar under the accumulated pressure of June and, by Friday, everything had been handled.

He thought about Lily finding her footing. Caroline's closing. The warm buyer lead he had passed with confidence. Watching someone else rise and feeling it as something more than satisfaction.

He thought about the cookout. Patricia's hug. The principal's handshake. The string lights in the oaks. Charlotte watching from the shade.

* * *

He pulled up the CRM and checked his pipeline.

He reviewed his calendar for the week.

Everything was in order. Every contact had a next action. Every open transaction had a clear path forward. The week ahead had structure — lead generation block in the morning, showing windows in the afternoon, a listing consultation on Thursday, follow-up time built into Wednesday. Nothing was squeezed. Nothing was guesswork.

It was working. Not because it ran itself — it didn't. It worked because he maintained it. Because every week, he showed up for the system the way he showed up for his clients: consistently, with full attention, without looking for reasons to skip.

He thought about what Charlotte had said once, in one of their earliest conversations about the foundation.

The foundation doesn't announce itself. It just holds everything.

That was the truth he now carried.

Consistent production. Fewer emotional swings. Stronger client relationships. A calendar that reflected priorities instead of chaos. Those weren't the glamorous outcomes people put in production screenshots or hung on walls. But they were the outcomes that made everything else possible — the life underneath the business, steady and supportable and real.

The foundation hadn't made the work easy.

It had made it manageable. Repeatable. Sustainable.

And those three words, he now understood, were the entire point.

* * *

He closed the laptop. He thought about the year ahead.

More listings. More consistency. More investment back into the business. He had told Charlotte as much in their December session, and he had meant it in a way he couldn't have meant it a year ago — not as ambition wearing the shape of a plan, but as an actual plan. Something to build toward with the same deliberate attention he'd given to everything that had brought him here.

He picked up his notebook and capped it.

Outside, the coast was fully light now.

The day was ready.

And so was he.

* * *

There was one more thing he thought about, sitting at that kitchen table.

He thought about what the foundation had made possible beyond the numbers. Not the income — though the income was real and meaningful and had changed what his days looked like in concrete ways. But the other things. The things that didn't appear on a P&L.

The fact that his phone could go quiet on a Sunday without fear rising in his chest. The fact that when a client called with a problem, he could listen to the full problem before responding instead of filtering it through the anxiety of what it might cost him. The fact that when a market shift happened — rates bouncing, inventory tightening, buyers hesitating — he didn't have to reinvent his entire approach. He just stayed consistent. He leaned harder into the warm touches. He made the calls. He trusted the system.

The business no longer consumed him.

It supported him.

That had been Charlotte's framing from the very beginning of Part IV: *the question becomes what kind of life does this make possible?* He had heard it then as something to work toward. Sitting here now, notebook on the table, coffee warm, the morning fully arrived outside the window, it was something he was already living.

A business that could grow without breaking. Weather markets without panic. Support a life instead of consuming it.

The foundation had done that quietly, holding everything he had built on top of it, never announcing itself, never demanding recognition.

Just holding.

* * *

FOUNDATION MARKER

Leadership Window: You only notice foundations when they fail. The strongest ones quietly hold everything you build on top of them. The agent who invests in structure — systems, discipline, relationships, leverage — rarely sees dramatic proof of its value, because the drama never comes. That absence of crisis is the return on the investment. That is the foundation working.

You should now understand:

- What a durable real estate business makes possible beyond production numbers — choices, margin, time, sustainability
- Why the foundation something you return to, not something you complete — it deepens with each cycle
- How consistent production, fewer emotional swings, and stronger client relationships are structural outcomes, not personality traits
- That growth compounds when you repeat the right inputs deliberately — not when you reinvent, but when you recommit
- That the goal was never success alone. It was sustainability: a business that could grow without breaking, weather markets without panic, and support a life instead of consuming it

* * *

CLOSING: Build Once, Adjust Often

* * *

Real estate will always change. Markets shift, technology evolves, and what clients expect tomorrow will look different from what they expect today. It's just the nature of the work. What doesn't change is the foundation beneath it all: clear systems, honest numbers, strong relationships, and the intentional choices that turn a busy career into a lasting business.

The work you've done here isn't something you finish. It's something you return to — when things feel heavy, when effort and direction stop lining up, when you catch yourself grinding without really building. The foundation isn't just a starting point. It's what allows you to keep going.

I didn't write this book because real estate needed another opinion. I wrote it because I've watched too many talented agents — the ones who genuinely care, who show up every single day, who have everything it takes — get stuck anyway. Not because they lacked hustle, but because no one had ever shown them how to put the pieces together. So, they improvised. They reacted. They carried everything themselves. And over time, even the best agents break under that weight.

This book is my attempt to change that, even in a small way.

The truth is you don't have to build alone. The resources around you — systems, support, tools, community — exist to protect your time and amplify what you're already good at. True freedom in this business doesn't come from doing everything yourself. It comes from building enough structure that your business stops consuming you and starts working for you. Clear numbers replace guesswork. Systems replace memory. Intentional days replace chaos.

I believe real estate can be both successful and deeply human. You can serve people well without burning out. You can grow without losing sight of why you started. You can build something steady even when the market isn't. Not perfectly — but consistently, and with intention.

You have everything you need to build something worth building. Trust the process, use what's in front of you, and protect what matters most. Let this be the business that supports the life you actually want.

It's yours to build.

— Dani

* * *

APPENDICES

Appendix A: Agent Priority & Time Management Worksheet

The Real Estate Eisenhower Matrix

This is the worksheet Charlotte handed Mason in Chapter 5 — the one she tapped on the table and said, "If it isn't scheduled, it isn't protected." He kept it on his desk from that week forward.

Why This Matters

Not all tasks are created equal, and your calendar will fill itself if you let it. This matrix helps you separate what demands attention now from what builds your business over time — and stops you from confusing busyness with productivity. As Mason learned in Chapter 5 (The Rhythm of the Day) and again in Chapter 14 (The Calendar War), protecting your time isn't a luxury. It's the job.

Use this worksheet at the start of each week to sort your workload, assign your energy deliberately, and keep the business-building work from getting crowded out by the urgent.

Q1: DO NOW — Urgent & Important (Deal Protectors)
Handle immediately. These are active, time-sensitive situations where delay has real consequences.

Examples

- Offer deadlines
- Inspection or appraisal issues
- Active negotiations
- Hot buyers or sellers ready to act

Your Q1 Tasks This Week

____

____

____

____

Q2: SCHEDULE — Important, Not Urgent (Business Builders)

Block time on your calendar. This quadrant builds your future — and it will always lose to Q1 if you don't protect it in advance.

Examples

- Lead generation
- Sphere follow-up
- CRM cleanup
- Market analysis
- Client events planning
- Mail farming prep

Your Q2 Priorities This Week

____

____

____

Time Block Scheduled:☐ Yes ☐ No ☐ Needs Adjustment

Q3: DELEGATE — Urgent, Not Important (Leverage Opportunities)

Systematize or hand off. These tasks feel productive but don't require your specific expertise. Build the habit of passing them down.

Examples

- Scheduling showings
- Transaction paperwork coordination
- Data entry
- Social media posting

Tasks to Delegate or Systematize

____

____

____

Who or What Handles This?☐ CCC / TC ☐ Automation ☐ SOP ☐ Outsource

Q4: REVIEW — Not Urgent, Not Important (Time Leaks)

Minimize or eliminate. These are the activities that feel like work but don't move the needle. Name them so you can see them clearly.

Examples

- Endless home searches without defined criteria
- Tire kickers without commitment or timeline
- Busywork disguised as productivity

Activities to Limit or Eliminate

____

____

____

Weekly Focus Check

Top 3 High-Value Actions This Week *(The 20% that creates 80% of your results)*

____

____

____

Daily Non-Negotiables☐ Conversations ☐ Follow-up ☐ CRM updates ☐ Client care

Reflection (End of Week)

What worked well this week?

____

____

What felt reactive instead of intentional?

____

____

What will I protect on my calendar next week?

____

____

If it isn't scheduled, it isn't protected. If it isn't important, it shouldn't steal your best hours.

Appendix B: Daily Routines & Weekly Blocks Worksheet (Agent Version)

This is the rhythm Mason built block by block through Parts I and II — the daily structure that kept him moving forward even when deals stalled, clients panicked, and the market shifted. It didn't look glamorous. It just worked.

Why This Matters

A business built on consistency beats one built on bursts of effort every time. The problem isn't motivation — it's structure. When your daily and weekly calendar has clear, defended blocks for the right activities, you stop relying on willpower to decide what to do next. You already know. This worksheet, rooted in Chapter 5 (The Rhythm of the Day), is the daily and weekly operating rhythm for agents who want to build something that holds.

Use it as a fillable guide each week. The goal isn't perfection — it's return.

Daily Non-Negotiable Routine

This happens every business day, no matter what. These are the floor, not the ceiling.

Morning Focus (Before Distractions)

☐ CRM review — what's active, what's due, what needs attention today

☐ Check tasks and follow-ups — clear and prioritize

☐ Review pipeline and priorities — know your day before it knows you

Daily Lead & Relationship Actions

☐ Conversations (calls, texts, face-to-face) talk to real people every day

☐ Sphere / warm touches — stay present in the lives of people who trust you

☐ Log notes and assign next task in CRM — never leave a contact without a next step

Client Care

☐ Active client updates — proactive outreach before they have to ask

☐ Contract or listing check-ins — know the status before your client does

☐ Problem prevention (not firefighting) — anticipate, don't react

Daily Admin Close-Out

☐ Update CRM — same day, every day

☐ Clear inbox — handle, delegate, or delete

☐ Prep for tomorrow — set yourself up to win the morning

Estimated Daily Time Commitment: ☐ 60 min ☐ 90 min ☐2+ hrs

Weekly Time Blocks

Block these on your calendar. Defend them. If something can move, it moves — these don't.

Business Building Blocks

- ☐ Lead generation
- ☐ Sphere nurturing
- ☐ Market research
- ☐ Marketing prep

Day(s): ________________________

Time(s): ________________________

Client Execution Blocks

- ☐ Showings
- ☐ Consultations
- ☐ Negotiations
- ☐ Listing appointments

Day(s): ________________________

Time(s): ________________________

Operations & Review

- ☐ CRM cleanup
- ☐ File and compliance check
- ☐ Metrics review

Day(s): ________________________

Time(s): ________________________

Pareto Check (80/20 Rule)

Top 3 Actions That Drive Most of Your Results

____

____

____

Low-Value Tasks to Reduce or Delegate

____

____

____

End-of-Week Reflection

What stayed consistent?

____

____

Where did I lose focus or time?

____

____

What will I protect on my calendar next week?

____

____

Consistency is more important than intensity. Show up the same way on the slow weeks as you do on the busy ones — that's what builds a business that lasts.

Appendix C: Daily Routines & Weekly Blocks (Leader Coaching Version)

This is the framework Charlotte used with every agent she developed – including Lily. She didn't coach effort. She coached structure. The conversations she had weren't about working harder. They were about building the scaffolding that makes consistent performance possible.

Purpose

Inconsistency in agents rarely comes from lack of effort – it comes from lack of structure. This worksheet is a coaching tool for team leaders, Directors of Operations, and coaches who are helping agents move from reactive to intentional. Use it in weekly one-on-ones to diagnose where structure is breaking down, identify delegation opportunities, and make specific, accountable commitments for the week ahead.

Agent Name: ______________________

Week of: __________________________

Daily Routine Assessment

Does this agent have a repeatable, protected daily operating rhythm?

- ☐ Has a defined morning start time and process
- ☐ Uses CRM daily — not occasionally
- ☐ Logs notes consistently and same day
- ☐ Assigns a next task for every contact, every time

Coach Notes:

Weekly Block Review

Business-Building Time

☐ Clearly scheduled on the calendar

☐ Protected from showings and admin overflow

☐ Actually honored — not just planned

Coach Prompt: *"Which blocks move the business forward even when nothing is urgent?"*

Agent Response:

____

____

Client Execution Load

☐ Appropriate for current pipeline size

☐ Not crowding out Q2 / business-building work

Coach Prompt: *"What would break first if your volume doubled tomorrow?"*

Agent Response:

____

____

Operations & Review Habits

☐ CRM maintained and current

☐ Files clean and compliant

☐ Metrics reviewed regularly

Coach Prompt: *"Where are you relying on memory instead of systems?"*

Agent Response:

____

Pareto Coaching Check

Top 20% Actions Identified by Agent

____

____

____

Coach Observation: ☐ Accurate ☐ Needs refinement

Notes:

____

____

Delegation & Leverage Check
What is this agent still doing that someone else could handle?

☐ Transaction coordination

☐ Scheduling

☐ Data entry

☐ Marketing execution

Coach Prompt: *"What are you doing right now that someone else could do better, faster, or more consistently than you?"*

Agent Response:

____

____

Next-Week Commitments

One specific habit to protect: ________________________

One specific block to defend: ________________________

One system to strengthen or document: ________________________

You don't coach effort. You coach structure. Structure creates consistency. Consistency creates confidence — and a business that doesn't depend on heroics to survive.

Appendix D: 90-Day Team Onboarding Companion

The bones of this framework came from Elias. Charlotte refined the edges. Together they built an onboarding process that didn't just orient new agents — it set them up to actually produce. This is the companion guide for agents joining a team and reading The Foundation alongside the work.

Purpose

This appendix is a structured onboarding and execution guide for agents joining a team. It aligns directly with the three-part arc of The Foundation — each 30-day phase corresponds to one part of the book — and provides clear expectations, rhythms, and checkpoints for agent and leader alike. The goal isn't to rush through it. The goal is to build something that holds.

How to Use This Appendix

- Read alongside the book over 90 days — one phase at a time
- Execute weekly, not perfectly
- Review progress with your Team Leader, DOO, or Coach at regular intervals
- Focus on consistency, not speed — the foundation has to cure before you can build on it

Days 1–30: Pouring the Foundation

Aligned with Part I of The Foundation (Chapters 1–7)

This phase is about establishing identity, building systems, and creating the daily rhythm that will carry everything else. Nothing fancy yet — just the groundwork.

Focus Areas

- Business clarity and professional identity
- CRM setup, tagging, and daily usage
- Financial awareness — know your numbers before the pressure hits
- Daily routines — build them now, before volume makes them feel optional

Weekly Expectations

- CRM fully built and contact database tagged

- Daily conversations logged every business day
- Burn rate calculated and written down
- Weekly schedule time-blocked and defended

Team Support

- DOO assists with systems setup and tool orientation
- CCC supports process orientation and workflow
- Leader provides weekly accountability check-in

Days 31–60: Framing the Business

Aligned with Part II of The Foundation (Chapters 8–13)

The structure is in place. Now you build the business-facing habits — pipeline discipline, client process mastery, and the first experiments with delegation.

Focus Areas

- Pipeline clarity — every contact has a status, a task, and a timeline
- Buyer and seller journeys — follow the process, every time
- Delegation and leverage — start identifying what shouldn't stay on your plate
- Metric awareness — know your numbers, not just your feelings about your numbers

Weekly Expectations

- CRM pipeline updated daily without exception
- Buyer and seller processes followed with consistency
- Delegation opportunities identified and discussed with leader
- Weekly review completed every Friday

Team Support

- CCC handles transaction coordination
- DOO supports workflow refinement as volume grows
- Leader coaches prioritization decisions and pipeline review

Days 61–90: Weight-Bearing Growth

Aligned with Part III of The Foundation (Chapters 14–19)

This is where the foundation gets tested. Volume increases. Time gets squeezed. The habits built in the first 60 days either hold — or they don't.

Focus Areas

- Consistent production under real workload pressure

- Time protection — Q2 work stays on the calendar even when Q1 is loud
- Market adaptability — reading the environment, not fighting it
- Confidence under load — trusting the systems you've built

Weekly Expectations

- Q2 business-building work protected on the calendar
- Referral conversations happening naturally, not as a campaign
- Marketing aligned with systems — no improvising
- Capacity recognized early — flag it before it becomes a crisis

Team Support

- Leader guides growth strategy and scaling decisions
- DOO adjusts systems to handle increasing volume
- CCC ensures client experience remains steady and consistent

Weekly Review Checklist

Use this every Friday. It takes less than ten minutes. It keeps you honest.

☐ CRM updated — every active contact has a current note and next task

☐ Tasks assigned to every contact in the pipeline

☐ Pipeline accurate — no wishful thinking, no stale entries ☐ Time blocks honored — or honestly assessed if not

☐ One system improved, documented, or strengthened this week

Leader Coaching Prompts

Use these in your weekly one-on-one with your agent. The goal is structure, not surveillance.

- Where did the agent default to reaction instead of intention this week?
- What system prevented chaos — and does the agent know that it did?
- What would break at higher volume? Is that being addressed now?
- What should be protected, defended, or rebuilt going into next week?

Completion Marker

At 90 days, a well-onboarded agent should be able to say — honestly — that they:

☐ Operate with confidence, not just effort

☐ Use systems instinctively, not occasionally

☐ Maintain consistent daily activity regardless of market noise ☐

Feel supported by the team, not overwhelmed by the volume ☐

Are prepared for the next stage of growth — and have already started building toward it

The Foundation doesn't end at 90 days. It just means the structure is solid enough to build on. That's the point — not to finish, but to be ready.

Appendix E: The Next 90 Days (Post-Onboarding Growth)

This is the framework Mason returned to after completing his initial ramp-up — the guide that helped him understand why growth after the foundation phase should feel steadier, not heavier.

Purpose

The first 90 days are about building the foundation. This phase is about trusting it. The goal of the next 90 days is not acceleration for acceleration's sake — it is sustainable, repeatable growth built on systems that are already in place. Agents who skip this phase and push too hard too fast often rebuild the same problems at higher volume.

Primary Focus Areas

During this phase, the shift is from building systems to refining them. The work looks less dramatic than the first 90 days. That is intentional.

- Deepen sphere relationships through consistent, low-pressure contact
- Increase listing confidence through repetition and preparation
- Expand price point intentionally, not reactively
- Protect time aggressively as demand increases
- Review metrics monthly and adjust based on data, not emotion

This phase emphasizes quality over quantity and consistency over intensity.

What This Phase Looks Like in Practice

Agents who are progressing well through this phase will begin to notice changes that are subtle but significant. The work starts to feel less like effort and more like rhythm.

Indicators of healthy progression:

- Less emotional reaction to market shifts
- Stronger confidence in consultations — both buyer and seller
- More predictable pipeline flow, with fewer surprises
- Earlier recognition of capacity limits before they become problems
- Referral conversations happening naturally, without manufactured urgency

Growth should feel steadier, not heavier. If it feels heavier, something in the system needs attention before adding volume.

Quarterly Rhythm

Structure beyond 90 days requires a rhythm that holds even when the market is loud or unpredictable. Use this framework as a repeating cycle:

- **Monthly:** Metric review and one intentional adjustment
- **Quarterly:** Full CRM cleanup and re-tagging; identify stale contacts and renew relationship momentum
- **Quarterly:** Relationship-first marketing refinement — evaluate what is reaching people and what is noise
- **Quarterly:** Strategic planning for the upcoming season — review goals, capacity, and what the business needs next

Leader Coaching Prompts

Use these in weekly or bi-weekly conversations with agents in this growth phase:

- Where has this agent improved consistency since completing onboarding?
- Which systems are holding up under increased volume — and which are starting to show cracks?
- Where is friction beginning to appear? Is it a system problem or a behavior problem?
- What should be refined in the current approach rather than replaced entirely?

Success Marker

At the end of this phase, the agent is operating from a different posture than they were 90 days prior. The measure is not production volume — it is professional steadiness.

An agent who has completed this phase successfully:

- Maintains consistent activity without burning out
- Uses systems instinctively rather than consciously
- Adjusts calmly when the market shifts instead of reacting emotionally
- Is prepared — and willing — to expand intentionally

The foundation was built in the first 90 days. This phase proves it holds weight.

Appendix F: One-Page Agent Metrics Tracker

Purpose

Track your key metrics weekly to make data-driven decisions.

Weekly Activity Metrics

Week Of: ______________________

Conversations Held: ______________________

Follow-Ups Scheduled: ______________________

Follow-Ups Completed: ______________________

Follow-Up Completion Rate: (Completed ÷ Scheduled) × 100 = ________ %

Pipeline Snapshot

Stage	**Count**
Leads	______________________
Attempting Contact	______________________
Hot	______________________
Warm	______________________
Under Contract	______________________
Past Clients	______________________

Conversion Check

Lead → Signed Conversion Rate: (Signed ÷ Leads) × 100 = ________ %

Contracts Written This Week: ______________________

Average Days from First Contact to Contract:

____

Weekly Adjustment

What input needs more attention next week?

____

____

Appendix G: Leader-Facing Metrics Scorecard

Purpose
Coach from structure, not frustration — let the numbers open the conversation.

Agent Name: ______________________
Week Of: ______________________

Activity Review
Conversations Held: ______________________ Target Met? ☐Yes ☐ No
Follow-Up Completion Rate: ________ % Target Met? ☐ Yes ☐ No

Coach Prompt: If conversations are low, is this a time problem, a priority problem, or an avoidance problem?

Pipeline Health
Overall Pipeline Status: ☐ Balanced ☐ Front-Heavy ☐ Mid-Heavy ☐ Thin

Coach Prompt: Which stage is weakest right now, and what behavior would change that over the next 30 days?

Conversion Review
Lead → Signed Conversion Rate: ________ %
Contracts Written This Week: ______________________

Coach Prompt: If conversion is low, is it a follow-up problem, a consultation problem, or a lead qualification problem?

Cycle Time
Average Days from First Contact to Contract:
____

Coach Prompt: Where in the process does momentum typically slow down?

Coaching Observations
Is this a consistency issue or a capability issue? ☐ Consistency ☐Capability ☐ Both

Primary Adjustment for Next Week
One specific change this agent will make:
____

Appendix H: Business Entity Basics

This is the conversation Mason had early in his career — the one Charlotte referenced— when she told him that showing up to work without a business structure is like building a house without a permit. And it is the mindset Elias returned to when Mason finally understood the difference between being self-employed and running a business.

Protecting What You're Building

This book focuses on operating your real estate business with clarity, structure, and intention. As your business grows, one of the most important foundational decisions you will make is how it is legally and financially set up.

This appendix is not legal or tax advice. It is an explanation of why formalizing your business matters — and the bare minimum steps most agents take to protect their assets and create clean financial separation. Every situation is different. Consult a qualified CPA and attorney before making any decisions specific to your circumstances.

Why Real Estate Agents Should Operate as a Business Entity

When you begin earning income in real estate, you are running a business whether you acknowledge it or not. The question is not whether you have a business. The question is how exposed it is.

Operating under a properly formed business entity can help you:

- Separate personal assets from business activity
- Reduce personal liability exposure
- Create clearer financial boundaries between your business and your personal life
- Support professional credibility with vendors, partners, and clients
- Simplify accounting, tax planning, and cash flow management

Real estate is a profession where contracts, money, and legal obligations intersect daily. Formalizing your business structure is not about complexity. It is about protection and clarity.

Many agents wait until something goes wrong to address this. The goal of this appendix is to help you address it before anything does.

Asset Protection and Financial Separation

One of the biggest risks agents face — especially in the early years — is commingling personal and business finances. It happens gradually and usually without intention. A commission gets deposited into a personal account. An expense gets charged to a personal card. The lines blur. The business becomes impossible to read clearly.

When income, expenses, and taxes flow through personal accounts:

- It becomes harder to track true profitability
- Mistakes are easier to make and harder to catch
- Personal assets may carry more exposure than necessary
- Stress increases significantly during tax season, audits, or business reviews

A separate business entity and bank account create a clear line between what belongs to the business and what belongs to you personally. That line is not a formality. It is a decision with real operational and legal consequences.

That separation supports better decisions, cleaner systems, and a business that is easier to manage, review, and grow.

The 5 Bare Minimum Steps to Formalize the Business

The following steps represent the basic framework most agents use — not a detailed how-to guide. Requirements vary by state and situation. Always consult a qualified CPA or attorney for advice specific to your circumstances before proceeding.

Step 1: Choose an Entity Type

Most agents work with a CPA or attorney to determine whether an LLC, S-Corp, or other entity structure is appropriate for their situation and state. The specifics of the right entity type depend on factors including income level, tax strategy, liability exposure, and long-term business goals.

The goal is not the label. The goal is liability protection and financial clarity. Choose the structure that serves both.

Step 2: Obtain an EIN

An Employer Identification Number (EIN) is issued by the IRS and functions like a Social Security number for your business. It is the federal identifier that makes your business entity real in the eyes of the government and financial institutions.

An EIN is commonly required to:

- Register your business with your state's entity department
- Open a business bank account
- File business tax documents
- Work with certain vendors, contractors, and partners

EINs are available directly through the IRS and are typically issued quickly. Your CPA or attorney can walk you through this step.

Step 3: Register the Entity With Your State

Once an entity type is chosen and an EIN is obtained, the business must be registered with your state's designated business registration department. This is usually the Secretary of State's office, though it varies by state.

This registration establishes your business as a legal entity separate from you personally. It is what makes the liability protection real rather than theoretical. Without it, the separation you are trying to create does not fully exist.

Requirements, fees, and renewal schedules vary by state. Your attorney can guide you through this process and confirm ongoing compliance requirements.

Step 4: Open a Business Checking Account

Once the entity is registered, open a business checking account in the name of the entity — not your personal name, and not a hybrid account. A dedicated business account is non-negotiable.

All income and expenses related to your real estate business should flow through this account. Every commission deposit. Every business expense. Every tax payment.

This step alone creates significant clarity. It makes your business legible to you, your accountant, and anyone else who ever needs to review it.

Step 5: Route All Business Activity Through the Business Account

Having the account is only useful if you use it consistently. Commissions, business expenses, taxes, and owner pay should all be handled intentionally through the business account.

This routing allows:

- Accurate tracking of profitability at any point during the year
- Cleaner implementation of financial systems like Profit First
- Reduced stress and confusion when reviewing numbers monthly or quarterly
- A clear picture of what the business actually costs to run and what it produces

Inconsistency here defeats the purpose of having the structure in the first place. The habit of routing everything through the business account is as important as the account itself.

How This Supports Everything in This Book

Formalizing the business is not an isolated administrative task. It directly supports the systems and frameworks taught throughout *The Foundation.*

A separate entity and business bank account make it easier to:

- Calculate your burn rate accurately
- Pay yourself intentionally and consistently, rather than from whatever is left
- Track true operating expenses without mixing in personal spending
- Review your metrics with confidence, knowing the numbers reflect reality
- Implement financial systems like Profit First without confusion or guesswork

- Make adjustments based on real data rather than estimates and assumptions

Without financial separation, systems become harder to trust. And when you cannot trust your systems, you default to instinct — which is expensive, inconsistent, and exhausting.

The business entity is not the most visible part of the foundation. But it is one of the most structurally important.

When to Do This

There is no single right moment to formalize a real estate business. Many agents choose to do it when:

- Income becomes consistent enough to justify the structure
- Business expenses begin to increase meaningfully
- They are preparing to make major financial commitments
- They begin implementing structured financial systems and want clean data to work with
- They realize that operating without separation is creating confusion or exposure

The longer this is delayed, the more complicated the cleanup tends to be. Commingled accounts, unclear expense records, and missing deductions are problems that compound over time.

There is no perfect time. There is only the moment when protecting what you are building becomes a priority.

Make that moment intentional.

Appendix I: 30/60/90-Day Self-Assessment

At each milestone — 30 days, 60 days, and 90 days — Mason set aside time to check in with himself honestly. Not to judge where he was, but to see clearly. Charlotte told him early on: you can't lead a business you won't look at. This is the assessment she handed him before he walked out of her office that first Monday morning.

Why This Matters

Progress in real estate is easy to feel without being able to measure. This self-assessment replaces vague impressions with honest checkpoints. Answer based on what you are actually doing — not what you intend to do, not what you did last month. Honest answers here are the foundation of real adjustment.

Answer each section based on your current execution, not intention.

30-Day Checkpoint: Foundation & Clarity

(Aligns with Part I — Chapters 1–7)

- ☐ I understand my burn rate and basic financial picture.
- ☐ My CRM is set up and used daily.
- ☐ Every contact has a next action assigned.
- ☐ I have established daily non-negotiables.
- ☐ My calendar reflects protected work time.

Reflection

What feels clearer than it did 30 days ago?

____

____

What still feels inconsistent?

____

____

One adjustment I will make next week:

____

____

60-Day Checkpoint: Flow & Systems

(Aligns with Part II — Chapters 8–13)

☐ My pipeline stages are clear and accurate.
☐ I follow a consistent buyer and seller process.
☐ I am using leverage appropriately — team, tools, or both.
☐ Follow-up happens without relying on memory.
☐ Weekly reviews guide my adjustments.

Reflection

Where has structure reduced stress?

____

____

Where am I still reacting instead of leading?

____

____

One system I will strengthen:

____

____

90-Day Checkpoint: Stability & Growth

(Aligns with Part III — Chapters 14–19)

☐ My activity is consistent regardless of market noise.
☐ I review metrics without avoidance.
☐ My time blocks are protected and realistic.
☐ Client experience remains steady during busy periods. ☐ I feel confident in my process and in the value I deliver.

Reflection

What has changed most in how my business feels?

____

____

What must be protected going forward?

____

____

One priority for the next 90 days:

____

____

Consistency is not a personality trait. It is a decision you make — and remake — every 30 days. Keep checking in.

Appendix J: Leader Implementation Guide

Charlotte didn't hand Mason the book and walk away. She walked through it with him — chapter by chapter, check-in by check-in. This guide is what she used behind the scenes: how she deployed the material, what she watched for at each phase, and how she kept herself from coaching personality when she should have been coaching structure.

Why This Matters

The Foundation works best when it is treated as a professional development framework, not optional reading. As a leader, how you deploy this book determines what your agents take from it. The goal is not speed. The goal is professional consistency — agents who execute reliably, not brilliantly and then not at all.

How to Deploy the Book

- **Introduce the book as a 90-day operating framework**, not optional reading. Set expectations clearly at the start: this is how we build here.
- **Pair chapters with weekly check-ins or team reviews.** The book is designed as a 12-week reading project — approximately two chapters per week. Let the chapters drive your conversation topics, not replace them.
- **Use appendices as working documents, not handouts.** Appendices A–K are tools. Have your agents fill them out, bring them to check-ins, and update them regularly.

This book works best when:

- Expectations are clear from day one
- Progress is reviewed regularly, not just at the end
- Structure is coached, not personality

What to Watch For by Phase

Early Phase (0–30 Days)

(Chapters 1–7 — Pouring the Foundation)

Watch For:

- Resistance to structure — the belief that systems are for other people

- Inconsistent CRM usage, or setup without daily engagement
- Overconfidence without clarity — energy in place of process

Coach:

- Daily non-negotiables and morning routines
- Financial awareness and burn rate calculation
- Task assignment discipline inside the CRM

Middle Phase (31–60 Days)

(Chapters 8–13 — Framing the Business)

Watch For:

- Follow-up drift — tasks scheduled but not completed
- Overbooking without protecting Q2 work
- Avoidance of metrics — looking busy instead of looking at numbers

Coach:

- Pipeline clarity and stage accuracy
- Time blocking and calendar protection
- Delegation opportunities — what can be handed off?

Later Phase (61–90 Days)

(Chapters 14–19 — Weight-Bearing Growth)

Watch For:

- Capacity strain — volume increasing, systems starting to crack
- Shortcutting systems that were working — reverting to reactive habits
- Emotional decision-making under load

Coach:

- Protection of Q2 work even when Q1 feels urgent
- Leverage utilization — team roles, tools, and support
- Calm execution under pressure; consistency is the standard

Leader Reminder

When performance dips, resist the instinct to address effort first.

Work through this sequence instead:

Check **consistency** before capability
Check **systems** before motivation

Check **structure** before effort

Most performance problems are not motivational — they are structural. Find the gap in the process before addressing the person.

This book creates professionals when used patiently. Hold the standard. Keep coaching the structure.

Appendix K: The 7-Day Foundation Reset

There were moments in Mason's story — and there will be moments in yours — when the business feels loud, scattered, and reactive. Work is happening, but nothing feels like it's actually moving. When that feeling arrives, this is the protocol. Seven days. Fifteen to thirty minutes each. A return to the fundamentals that hold everything else up.

Why This Matters

Busy is not the same as productive. This reset is not about doing more — it is about returning to the right things, done consistently. One focused week can shift the entire feel of a business. Each day requires only 15–30 minutes. Consistency matters more than perfection.

Day 1: Calculate Your Burn Rate

(15 minutes — See Chapter 4: The Real Cost of Showing Up)

Determine what it costs your business to exist each month. Not what you want to earn — what it costs to operate before a dollar of profit arrives.

Include:

- All business expenses (marketing, technology, licensing, support)
- Personal income needs (rent, food, transportation, obligations)
- Owner pay and any tax reserves

My current monthly burn rate: $______________________

Outcome: You stop guessing and start making decisions from clarity.

Day 2: Clean 50 CRM Contacts

(See Chapter 3: The System Nobody Sees)

Select 50 contacts in your CRM and complete the following for each:

- Update contact information (phone, email, address)
- Add notes from the last interaction
- Assign a next action with a specific due date

No next action = no relationship momentum. A database without next actions is just a list.

Outcome: Your database becomes active, not passive.

Day 3: Block Your Calendar — Protect Q2 Work

(See Chapter 5: The Rhythm of the Day and Chapter 14: The Calendar War)

Time block your upcoming week with intention. Before anything else fills the calendar, protect:

- Lead generation blocks
- Follow-up windows
- Relationship-building time (sphere calls, lunches, referral partners)

Work ON your business before working IN it.

Outcome: Your calendar reflects your priorities, not the loudest urgency of the moment.

Day 4: Make 20 Sphere Calls

(See Chapter 6: The Conversation That Counts)

Reach out to 20 people you already know. These are not sales calls — they are human ones.

- Check in genuinely
- Offer help if it fits
- Stay present and curious; let the conversation lead

No scripts required. Care creates opportunity.

Outcome: Relationships are strengthened without pressure or agenda.

Day 5: Review Your Numbers and Pipeline

(See Chapter 12: The Numbers and Chapter 8: The Pipeline)

Pull up your metrics and pipeline and spend 20 minutes looking at the full picture.

Review:

- Active and upcoming transactions
- Pipeline strength across all stages (Hot / Warm / Nurture)
- Upcoming opportunities and next steps

Ask yourself:

- What's moving?
- What needs attention this week?
- What's missing from my pipeline right now?

Outcome: You lead your business instead of reacting to it.

Day 6: Refine One Process

(See Chapter 11: The Handoff and Chapter 19: The Standard)

Choose one process you already use and make it better. Not a full rebuild — a refinement.

Options:

- Buyer consultation flow
- Seller consultation and listing prep
- Follow-up sequence
- Transaction handoff to TC

Do not rebuild. Refine. Small improvements compound quickly, and a cleaner process is a more confident process.

Outcome: Small improvements compound quickly.

Day 7: Plan for the Next Week

(See Chapter 5: The Rhythm of the Day)

End the reset looking forward, not backward. Take 20 minutes to review the week and set up what comes next.

Plan:

- Next week's time blocks
- Priority conversations and follow-ups
- Any unfinished items from this reset week

Review what worked. Adjust what didn't. End the week prepared, not depleted.

Outcome: Momentum carries forward instead of resetting every Monday morning.

Final Note

This reset is not about doing more.

It is about doing the right things, consistently — the same fundamentals that Mason returned to every time the noise got loud. Repeat this rhythm whenever your business feels reactive, scattered, or stalled.

Foundations are built one intentional step at a time. So are comebacks.

Glossary of Terms

The language of a well-run business matters. These terms appear throughout The Foundation and are used with intention. Understanding them is part of building with clarity.

Activity Metrics

Quantitative measures of daily and weekly actions taken by the agent — conversations initiated, follow-ups completed, appointments set, and similar trackable behaviors. In *The Foundation*, activity metrics are leading indicators: they reveal what's happening before results either rise or decline.

Average Days to Contract

The average number of days between first meaningful contact with a client and going under contract. This metric helps identify delays in process, follow-up, or confidence — not effort alone. Tracked as part of the metrics review.

Burn Rate

The amount of money your business requires each month to operate before paying yourself. Burn rate creates financial awareness and informs decisions about expenses, pricing, and leverage.

Business Entity

A legally recognized structure — such as an LLC — used to separate personal and business finances and activity. In *The Foundation*, the emphasis is on asset protection and financial clarity, not tax optimization alone.

CCC (Client Care Coordinator)

A team role responsible for managing the full arc of the client experience — from contract-to-close coordination through long-term relationship management. The CCC handles transaction timelines, documents, lender and attorney coordination, and post-closing follow-up, protecting agent time and ensuring consistency across every client touchpoint. Maya Ellis serves in this role throughout the story.

Closing Rate
The percentage of signed clients who successfully reach closing. Used to evaluate transaction management and client alignment — not sales skill alone. A healthy closing rate reflects both process and communication.

Commission Split
The percentage of commission allocated between the agent, team, brokerage, and franchise (if applicable). In *The Foundation*, commission splits are examined to understand true income and real margin — not to compare compensation models.

Conversation
A meaningful two-way interaction related to real estate, including phone calls, in-person meetings, or substantive text exchanges. Conversations are tracked as an activity metric and treated as the primary driver of pipeline momentum.

Conversion Rate
The percentage of contacts that move from one stage of the pipeline to the next. Conversion rates highlight process strength or weakness — where the business flows and where it stalls.

CRM (Customer Relationship Management) The system used to track contacts, conversations, tasks, and follow-up. In *The Foundation*, the CRM replaces memory and protects relationships. A CRM without consistent use is not a system — it is a list.

DOO (Director of Operations)
A leadership role responsible for systems, workflows, and operational efficiency on a team. The DOO helps stabilize the business as volume increases, allowing agents and leaders to focus on revenue-generating work. Elias Bennett serves as DOO throughout the story.

EIN (Employer Identification Number)
A federal tax identification number issued by the IRS for a business entity. It enables financial separation and is required for professional business operations under a registered entity.

Eisenhower Matrix
A prioritization framework that categorizes tasks by urgency and importance. Adapted throughout *The Foundation* to help agents protect time, identify leverage opportunities, and reduce the feeling of constant overwhelm. The four quadrants are labeled Q1–Q4 in this book.

Follow-Up
Intentional contact with a person already in the CRM, scheduled with a clear purpose and a specific date. In *The Foundation*, follow-up is planned and tracked — not reactive or memory-dependent. Consistent follow-up is treated as a professional standard, not an optional habit.

Follow-Up Completion Rate
The percentage of scheduled follow-ups that are actually completed.

Formula: Completed Follow-Ups ÷ Scheduled Follow-Ups × 100

This metric reveals consistency and discipline more accurately than any production number. Introduced in Chapter 12: The Numbers.

GCI (Gross Commission Income)
The total commission earned before any splits or expenses. GCI is a top-line production number — useful for understanding volume but not a reliable indicator of business health or take-home income.

Hot / Warm / Nurture
Pipeline categories that describe a contact's readiness to make a real estate decision:

- **Hot** — Actively making a decision now
- **Warm** — Interested, but timing is unclear
- **Nurture** — Long-term relationship; not yet in motion

Lead
A contact who has expressed interest in real estate but has not yet committed to working with an agent. Leads require consistent follow-up and a clear process to move toward a signed agreement.

Lead-to-Signed Conversion Rate
The percentage of leads that become signed clients.

Formula: Signed Clients ÷ Leads × 100

Used to evaluate consultation effectiveness and follow-up quality — not raw effort or number of attempts.

Leverage

The strategic use of people, systems, or tools to handle tasks that do not require the agent's personal involvement. Leverage exists to protect relationships, energy, and the agent's highest-value time. Introduced in Chapter 11: The Handoff.

Metrics

Numerical indicators used to evaluate activity, consistency, and outcomes over time. In *The Foundation*, metrics are treated as diagnostic tools — not judgment. They show where the business is working and where it needs attention.

Net Income

What remains after all expenses, taxes, and owner pay have been accounted for. Net income reflects business health more accurately than production volume alone. A high-GCI agent with no net income has a revenue problem, not a production one.

Next Action

The specific, scheduled task assigned to a contact in the CRM — the exact step that keeps a relationship moving forward. Every contact should always have a next action. A contact without a next action is a relationship at risk of being forgotten.

Operating Expenses

The costs required to run the business: marketing, technology, licensing, insurance, support services, and similar recurring obligations. Operating expenses are managed intentionally to support long-term sustainability, not minimized arbitrarily.

Owner Pay

The amount the business pays the agent as consistent personal income. Owner pay is planned and intentional — not whatever is left after expenses. Treating it as a fixed obligation creates financial discipline and business clarity.

Pareto Principle (80/20 Rule)
The observation that a small percentage of actions produce the majority of results. Used throughout *The Foundation* to help agents identify and protect their highest-leverage activities — and stop over-investing in low-return work.

Pipeline
A visual representation of where contacts and clients are in the sales process, organized by stage. Pipeline clarity reduces emotional decision-making and improves prioritization.

Pipeline Health
A qualitative assessment of balance and depth across pipeline stages. A healthy pipeline is not overly dependent on one stage, one client, or one source. Pipeline health is reviewed as part of the weekly review practice.

Profit First
A financial framework, developed by Mike Michalowicz, that prioritizes profit, owner pay, and taxes before operating expenses are paid. Used in *The Foundation* to encourage intentional money management and prevent the common pattern of spending whatever remains.

Q1 / Q2 / Q3 / Q4 Work
Task categories derived from the Eisenhower Matrix, used throughout *The Foundation* to guide prioritization:

- **Q1 (Quadrant 1):** Urgent and important — active deal protection, client crises, deadlines
- **Q2 (Quadrant 2):** Important, not urgent, lead generation, relationship-building, business development. Q2 work builds the business. Protecting it is crucial.
- **Q3 (Quadrant 3):** Urgent, not important — interruptions, low- value requests, delegation opportunities
- **Q4 (Quadrant 4):** Neither urgent nor important — time leaks, scrolling, busywork

Sphere

Your personal and professional network — people who know you, like you, and trust you. In *The Foundation*, the sphere is treated as a long-term asset, not a sales list. Consistent, genuine care for your sphere generates referrals without pressure.

Systems

Repeatable processes that replace memory and reduce variability in how work gets done. Systems enable consistent client experiences, scalable growth, and a business that does not depend entirely on one person's daily presence.

Time Blocking

The practice of assigning specific, protected blocks of time on the calendar for defined activities. Time blocking ensures that important work — particularly Q2 work — is done before urgency fills the day.

Transaction Coordinator (TC)

A role responsible for managing contract documents, compliance, deadlines, and communication once a transaction goes under contract. In *The Foundation*, this function is handled by the Client Care Coordinator (Maya Ellis), who manages both transaction coordination and long-term client relationships. In many teams, this may be a separate dedicated role — either way, it represents one of the highest-leverage support functions available to a growing agent.

Under Contract

The stage in a real estate transaction where both buyer and seller have signed a purchase agreement and the transaction is progressing through due diligence, financing, and closing steps.

Weekly Review

A recurring, scheduled review of activity metrics, pipeline status, upcoming follow-ups, and time usage from the prior week. Weekly reviews drive intentional adjustment and prevent the slow drift that happens when a business runs on momentum alone

Weight-Bearing Growth
Growth that occurs after systems, processes, and support structures are established — allowing increased volume without chaos, quality decline, or burnout.

About the Author

Dani Landers has spent her career at the intersection of sales and operations — where the real work of building a business gets done. As Director of Operations for a real estate team and Principal Consultant at Willowcross Consulting, she brings a rare combination of frontline sales experience and deep operational expertise — the kind that comes from knowing both how business is won and how it's sustained.

She's spent years studying what separates thriving real estate businesses from ones that stay stuck in reactive mode: the systems, workflows, and financial structures that create consistency instead of chaos. Her gift is helping agents and team leaders see what's working, what's quietly costing them, and what needs to be built before the next level of growth becomes possible — and she has a knack for finding creative solutions where others see only obstacles.

The Foundation: Building a Real Estate Career That Stands Strong grew out of everything Dani has learned — and everything she's watched agents struggle to find on their own. It's written for anyone stepping into this business who wants to build it right from the start, with the belief that success isn't accidental. It's built on purpose, layer by layer, through the right habits, the right systems, and the kind of character that makes it last.

Dani lives and works along the coast of North Carolina, where she mentors agents and helps business owners build businesses that can truly sustain and support them.

Share your success stories! Info@WillowcrossConsulting.com

www.ingramcontent.com/pod-product-compliance
Lightning Source LLC
LaVergne TN
LVHW020710110826
845149LV00012B/2188

* 9 7 9 8 9 9 5 6 4 0 7 2 1 *